MW01233719

A Southern Black Woman Beats the Odds

As Told by Edith S. Childs

A Southern Black Woman
Beats the Odds

As Told

By

Edith S. Childs

6/6/2011.

*To Lovota (Bo) + Carolyn Abrams
(my friends) - Thank you so much for
your Kindnen - God bless.
EL*

Voice of Truths, LLC
Donalds, South Carolina

Published by:

Voice of Truths, LLC
Post Office Box 34
Donalds, SC 29638-0034
Email: publishers@voiceoftruths.com
Telephone: 864.302.0048
Fax: 864.392.9000
Website: www.voiceoftruths.com/

A Southern Black Woman Beats the Odds
Copyrighted © by Edith S. Childs

All rights are reserved. No part of this book may be reproduced in any form or by any means, electronically or mechanically including photocopying, recording or maintained in any type of informational storage and retrieval system without permission in writing from the copyright owner and the publisher. All inquiries must be addressed to the publisher.

The library of Congress Publication in Data

ISBN:978-0-9818992-6-8

Library of Congress Cataloging Number
2011926925

Editor: Kenneth N. Mufuka, PhD.
Graphics & Illustrations: Jason Cunningham
Layout by: VOTS

Voice of Truths is dedicated to the publication of quality works in the written word. The philosophy of Voice of Truths stands firmly fixed in the promotion of truth and regard. We want to make available for our readers well-documented literature that is written solely for their appreciation. This does not in anyway eliminate fictional genres of writing forms. We are interested in evaluating manuscripts for publication that encourage our aims. We seek writers of various styles.

Manufactured in the United States of America

A Southern Black Woman

Beats the Odds

As Told by Edith S. Childs

CONTENTS
Preface   9
Dedication   11

PREFACE:

It's been often said that the women of the house are our true CEO's. In the business world, these positions are normally filled by men. However, in the case of Edith S. Childs, it is clear she is an exception to the norm. She is an over-the-top person. She successfully holds down her CEO position at home while still performing well as a member of Greenwood's County Council. In addition, when it comes to wearing the many hats that are required of her, Edith is one of few that does it as well as she does. Literally, Mrs. Childs loves her hats and wears them rather well.

Edith was born October 11, 1948 in Greenwood, South Carolina as Edith Sanders. Her parents are Mrs. Ida Edwards and Mr. David Johnson. Edith is the third born of six siblings. She has four brothers: Marion (deceased 1960), James, Nathaniel, David and a sister, Ann. Edith is married to Charles Childs.

Edith and Charles are the proud parents of three children: Linda (Jeannie), Jerome and Larmont Childs. They also have six grandchildren: Lindaya, Lakeyia & Lorenzo Zobe Brown II, Jordan, Kequan & Cameron Childs.

Mrs. Childs reveals her life to the world so everyone can see her struggles and how she overcame them. Read about her life's triumphs as well as her failures. Her book tells the story of how *A Southern Black Woman Beats the Odds* and has a successful life.

The odds of success were set against being black. Of course being black was one obstacle, however, Edith is a black female that lives in the south. For her, life was not easy—she was determined to win life over. There were many nay-sayers that spoke words over her that she would never amount to anything. Despite all that was said and did against Mrs. Childs, her grandmother, Miss Mary Scurry displayed a solid faith in her by telling her daily, "One day Edith, you will be somebody uptown with those big folks." Even in her youth, Mrs. Childs' grandmother saw something that Edith was unaware of herself.

Hopefully, this book with its brief peek into the life of Edith S. Childs will warm your hearts, make you laugh and make you cry. Most important, you will know that God is the main source of her strength. He has allowed her to do many things. Mrs. Child says, "God will enable her to aspire in the future."

Sit back and enjoy as Mrs. Edith S. Childs' life unfolds before you.

Dedications

I dedicate this book to my family and to the people of Greenwood, South Carolina for their support through the years.

CHAPTER-ONE
Early Years

My mother was not a member of the National Association for the Advancement of Colored People (NAACP), nor was my grandmother. We did not know much about the Negro College Fund. None of my family was politically minded. Brewer Normal School provided the most advanced education for Negroes, and their teachers were called professors. But there was no doubt that 1948 was a favorable year for my family. I was born on a cold wintry day. A midwife delivered me. Her name was Miss Maggie Gary. I was born in my grandmother's home. Neither my mom nor my grandmother could afford for me to be born in Brewer Hospital.

Brewer Hospital was a facility reserved for African Americans. It was located next door to Brewer Normal School. Yes, there were black nurses that worked there and even a black doctor. I do not know where the doctor or the nurses were trained. I knew there was a world reserved for blacks and another bigger and better world for whites. All the same, change was in the air. Everyone pretty much so knew this. Talk was constant about the upcoming changes to Negro life.

Black soldiers were returning home from Europe. Many had fought in France, Germany and Britain. I will never know if the stories these soldiers talked about were exaggerated or not. I knew for certain that my Uncle Jack was in the United States Army. We were proud of him. He came home when he was on leave... his uniforms were always masterfully prepared... his pants were always cut with crisp creases. Uncle Jack was adorned with many awards he had earned from his overseas tours of duty. He looked dashing as a soldier. When he was home, he rode me around town in his shiny new car and took me to places away from home. I was especially proud of Uncle Jack. He remains my favorite uncle even to this day. Yes, there was change in the air.

I have two brothers that are older than I am. My grandmother, Mary Scurry assessed our situation soon after I was born. She was decisive and a very strong black woman. She was accustomed to making critical decisions. My grandma was upset that my mother could barely take care of herself, yet she continued to have children that she could not physically provide for, let alone place a roof over their heads. So grandma Mary told my mother in a soft but authoritative voice, "Child, you are in no condition to put a roof over these children's head. You go on and find yourself a job. Until you are able to provide stability for these babies and yourself, they will stay with me." And that was that. Once my grandma said what was what, there were no more words to be said.

I knew very little about my father. I do, however, recall having been slightly introduced to him. My father remains a faraway figure in the shadows of my life. There has been absolutely nothing between us, to separate us or to keep us together. He was simply not in the picture. I do not know why. I guess I will never know very much about what he did for a living or did not do. He died, and we never built a relationship with each other. Therefore, nothing was lost and nothing was gained. It is kind of funny, nowadays you hear of children who were abandoned or adopted, trying to find their long lost family members. In the case of my father and I, I really do not have any desires to know what he was about. I cannot see the benefit of it.

Grandma Mary was the whole world to me. My world started with her and ended with her. Every word that proceeded out of her mouth was the Law of Moses to me. She was loveable yet she was stern. She was not accustomed to being crossed by anyone, especially my brothers or me. We had the fear of God in us and knew not to cross her. If we did, we quickly learned our worlds would be turned upside down and inside out. So I learned at a very early age to do what I was told to keep the peace. If I did what I was told, I did not have to worry about repercussions. It was as if the spiritual balance of the universe had been tilted if we had been disobedient.

Grandma Mary had the best job in the world. She was the head cook at one of the local boarding houses. A white man owned the boarding house, which was just off Cambridge and Cokesbury Street. He rented rooms to boarders, who worked in town. Some stayed for very long periods of time while others stayed for shorter periods. Before 6am every morning, my grandmother got up and prepared breakfast for us before she went to work. After which, she went to the boarding house to cook for the boarders before they went to work. She worked the entire day, even though she came home midday sometimes to rest. She always walked to and from work, so she would be very tired when she came home in the evenings.

Since my grandmother was a cook, she made sure that she brought us the best food from the boarding house. There was never a time when we went without food. She used to boast about it. She called it putting food on the children's table. Looking back over those times now, we were very blessed. I knew that some of our neighbors complained that groceries were expensive, and they went with little food, especially toward the end of the month. Most of the older parents were paid at the end of the month.

The neighborhood children knew we always had food. They would hang out and pretend that they were our best friends so they could have dinner at our house. We knew they always timed it when our grandma would return home with a bag full of food and find them on our porch. They knew that grandma would never feed us and not feed them.

On Sunday, we ate late because grandma spent a lot of time at church. Church services lasted for three hours or more. Nobody seemed to be in a hurry to get out of church or to go home. Sunday was definitely God's day and that was it. There was no such thing as missing church unless you really had a good reason. Our grandmother was always the one to determine if that reason was ever good enough. We were never bored in church either, as we wore our Sunday's best. This was the only day we were allowed to wear our best unless we were going to what grandma called an occasion.

I will remember this one particular Sunday as long as I live. It was the beginning of my public awareness. I was playing in the streets with Lydia, a girl from the neighborhood. I said earlier that our friends used to hang around until our grandmother called us for Sunday dinner. They knew if I did not call them that grandma would look outside her kitchen door and ask, "Why are your friends staying outside? You know we have enough for everybody." At times, I really wondered if we did have enough for everybody. Sometimes I looked at the dinner table with a questioning eye. "Grandma, we do not have enough for ourselves," I stated. My grandma just brushed it aside with a sigh and went on about her way as if she did not see or hear me.

If grandma answered me, she would say, "Girl, I done told you, go out and call your friends. We will share what we have!" Of course, I had to do what I was told.

Anyway, this particular Sunday was a little different from the usual Sunday after church. Among us kids there weren't any differentiation of color that I recall. There were light-skinned black kids and some had in-between shades, while others were kind of light paper bag brown. I was of the natural African color. On this particular day, my friend Lydia looked at me with a look I had never seen before. She had challenged me to a race to the post, of course, I beat her. When Lydia caught her breath, she challenged me again. Once again, I beat her fair and square running to the post.

In a wild angry rage, Lydia said some bad words that I had never heard before. "You black ...!" she said. Yes, I heard those words. She said those words with such venom and disgust. I felt those words were supposed to hurt me, and they really did. People who think of the idiom sticks and stones may break my bones but words will never hurt me are entirely wrong.

Lydia's words were sharper than a doubled edged razor that is used to shave with. I felt those words cutting deep like a sharp knife slicing into my heart.

I said to Lydia, "Girl, what did you say?" I was now fuming with anger. Slowly and as calm as a viper that was ready to strike, I moved toward her. Once more I asked, "What did you say Lydia?" She repeated the words. By that time, I was within striking distance. I slapped her across the left side of her face with my opened right palm causing her to fall to the ground.

She was bleeding from her nose. Her bleeding was not enough to stop me from continuing my onslaught.

At that very moment, her mother was racing toward us. At first I thought their dinner was ready. I was not sure or not if she saw me hit Lydia. However, the result was not very good. Lydia's mother cried out in horror. "Stop hitting my child!" she said. She kept on running to where we were fighting. She pulled us apart and said, "You struck my child!"

I waited for what I knew was to come. My grandma always taught us that whenever you did something bad, you better wait right there for your punishment. She would say, "There is no use in running away. You know there is nowhere to hide in this world. Your sins will find you out. The sooner you own up to them, the better it will be for everybody." So I patiently waited for my punishment.

What came afterwards truly shocked me. I tried to tell Lydia's mother that Lydia had called me bad names. She wasn't in any mood to hear what I was saying. Lydia was crying and screaming as if I had torn her head off her body. Her mother lifted her precious from the ground. In my opinion, Lydia could have won an Academy Award for her performance. She really put on a show for her mother. Lydia was making the most horrible fuss as if she had been beaten within an inch of her life. I did not even get to do all that I wanted to do to her.

Lydia's mother shouted, "I have told you child not to mess with these Negroes." She said these words with an air of superiority.

"Child, do you hear me! From now on you leave these Negroes alone. If you don't play with them, they surely won't play with you," she continued.

At the time, I could not fathom the meaning of what Lydia's mother was saying. I was really confused about her attitude. What I was hearing was that she was actually putting me down. If I told my grandmother, she may want to fight Lydia's mother. Definitely, something was wrong with the way Lydia's mother pronounced the word Negro. All this was beyond me. Lydia's mother was acting out just because Lydia and I had a little fight. This was something that happened in our neighborhood all the time. The kids always fought with each other.

I never heard those kinds of words before Lydia said them to me. None of the other kids had ever said anything like this before. And in this case, it was all about a little fight.

More important, my immediate concern was how and when to break the news to my grandmother. I knew Lydia's mother was going to make a terrible fuss out of our fight. Her mom's actions portrayed a person who thought they were better than we were, or that they were two grades above all the other people who lived in the neighborhood .

Why did she think so? I just didn't know. I had no idea what my grandma would think, say or do. I did suspect that I was going to get a smack down because another adult had to discipline me. I thought that my reaction to Lydia's insult was the right and proper one, and that I was not to blame. What really mattered now was how my grandmother was going to view our little fight.

Surprisingly, grandma had been standing in the front doorway of the house as Lydia and I were fighting. She had seen everything. Grandma also saw how Lydia was wallowing in the dirt, crying and acting out as if she was being killed. But did grandma see everything that happened? I was not in a position to say, to ask or to think about it. Worse still, Lydia's mother was now walking toward the house with her little precious in tow. I knew what her position was going to be as she strutted like a peacock toward grandma.

Grandma remained as calm as a rock. She was still dressed in her Sunday best. She was still wearing her hat, and of course her high heel shoes and compulsory hosiery. She had told me in her lighter moments, "A Lady is not fully dressed unless she is adorned with a hat and her hosiery." She must have told me that a million times. More than fifty years later, I still feel the same way she felt about total dressing... may her soul rest in peace.

The moment was filled with possibilities, and I did not know which way the wind was going to blow. "Bring my switch," grandma ordered my older brother. My older brother and I rarely saw eye to eye on things. With grandma asking him to find a switch for her to use against me, I suspect it gave him the utmost pleasure. I was certain he truly relished the moment of choosing a switch.

I feared that I was going to be punished for slapping Lydia without a hearing. Where was grandma's sense of justice? Certainly, in this case she saw everything that had happened, and that I was just defending myself.

My grandma always wanted to be ready whenever she had to deal with children acting up. Usually, she would give each child a minute to state their case. She decided then and there who was wrong, and sometimes she decided that both kids were wrong. She would draw her switch and give a few good swats. We had to stand there and take it or get a really good whipping with that hickory switch. After we got our whopping, grandma would say, "Now you go on; let me not hear any more of this foolishness."

Lydia's mother was ready for war. She was also in her Sunday dress. Her scarf was flying in the wind while her left hand held her hat in place. Her right hand was pulling Lydia along as if she was an exhibit. She was intent on forcing my grandmother to confess wrong doing on my behalf. My grandma had witnessed the entire fight from her kitchen to her front door. Lydia's mother was screaming and calming down was out of the question. She was in an awful rage. Grandma gazed at her with a blank look on her face as if to say "who do you think you are approaching like that?"

"You gotta teach your little picaninny proper behavior and manners," screamed Lydia's mother.

"What did you say?" asked grandma.

"Your child just beat up on my little one. I done told Lydia, a long time ago, not to play with you Negroes. The girl won't listen to me." Lydia's mother did not finish her sentence. Lydia's mother said those ill-famed words again.

I never saw my grandma get so angry in all my life. Of course, I was just six-years-old at the time, but I recall every detail. Grandma acted as if she wanted to leap on top of Lydia's mother. Her eyes were on fire!

Filled with anger and shock, grandma asked one question, "Who you calling Negro? My little baby is going to be somebody one day. We will see then whom you calling a picaninny. Take care of your own picaninny."

Lydia's mother saw grandma's switch flying in the wind. She must have suspected that it was for her. She speedily changed courses but the switch fell squarely on her neck, snatching her Sunday scarf off. Grandma was in a good old rage now, and would have delivered another blast, but Lydia's mother was in full flight. Grandma could not chase her because of her age. Lydia's mother was younger and more nimble of the foot. She quickly sped home to safety.

I went into the house, to my room, and shut the door. It was about two hours later when my grandmother tapped softly on my door. "Come, my baby. Have something to eat. We saved something for you."

Grandma spoke in a soft voice, "Edith, remember this. Don't let nobody pull you into the gutter. You are going to be somebody one of these old days. If you ain't somebody, as the Lord liveth in this house, you gotta act like you are somebody." Her words were soft and gentle. They were said with such intensity and meaning that they ran down my spine.

This was my very first experience with outright oppression. And this oppression came from a black girl and her mother. Lydia was merely a lighter skin tone than me. Nonetheless, Lydia called me a black... as if being black meant that a person was defective or something.

Come to think of it, her mother was dark also. However, she seemed to flaunt Lydia's lighter skin tone as if she had accomplished something by having brought into this world a child with a lighter skin tone. Lydia's mother must have thought of it as a supreme achievement.

Why did the word black provoke such animosity in me, and a feeling of ill will that aroused inner hostilities? When Lydia said those words to me, I felt the hurt it conveyed. But when Lydia's mother said it to my grandmother, the whole world exploded.

The word black was a summation of everything that depicted evil and dirty that had befallen our race. So, I understood that something was wrong. Even at that young age, I understood that something was not right with the way they both said it. I read the oppression that came from within our race because of what the word black was supposed to confer. However, my first oppressor was Lydia and her mother, who were also black. The weapon used in this oppression was the shade of my skin. I was completely baffled as how to combat this evil that lived within our people.

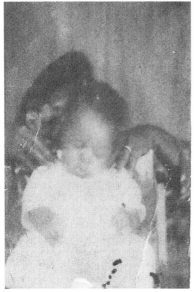

Baby Edith about three months old.

Little Edith age three sitting on steps at the Pecan Orchard home.

From left to right: sister Ann, brother David, Aunt Linda and grandma Mary Scurry-(deceased).
Top row L-R: brother James, Marion, (deceased) Edith, Nate (bowtie).

Edith during her first year in school.

CHAPTER-TWO
Early Years II

We lived at Pecan Orchard Estates. It was a death wish to disrespect any adults living there. Some big boys at times bullied smaller kids. They did not get away with bullying all the time. An older boy, about ten or so, would say to a younger boy, who was about six or so, "Give me your biscuits!" Of course the six-year-old did not give up his biscuits so both of them ended up fighting.

One may ask, "Why did the little kid fight? He should have known he was going to get whipped?" Simply, the answer is if the little boy does not fight for what is his, he will have nothing in the future. The bully must pay some kind of price for what he is taking. This must be established so he will know, at least, he must calculate the cost of bullying with anyone else.

If it is another six-year-old boy, or for that matter, any age, the bully will know that he will have to fight even if he has already whipped the boy once. The point here is you must fight any way and at all cost. You just cannot give in to the pressures of life. Even at an early age, you must learn this fact or you will be swallowed up by the bullish part of life. Fighting was part of my life as a child, and I was accustomed to it.

Lydia and I were now friends. Together we decided to attend a homecoming football game. I do not recall how we became friends; it was something that just happened. After my grandmother's incident with Lydia's mother, we maintained the peace treaty. For a while we had been hanging out together. Nonetheless, we went to the homecoming football game. We had a good time.

After the homecoming game, dinner was served at Mt. Pisgah African Methodist Episcopal Church (AME) in Greenwood. This was the tradition.

My grandma was surprised to see us coming home from church together laughing and talking. She called me aside. "Is everything all right?" She asked me with concern in her voice.

"Yes. Why do you ask grandma?" I inquired.

"You know how to take care of yourself don't you?" She said this with resolve of voice. We read each other perfectly.

"Nobody is going to disrespect you, Edith. You hear me!" That was a command.

"Was everything all right at that church?" she asked

again. Grandma had asked me that question before.

"Why do you ask?" I inquired in frustration.

"Did you eat anything?" The questioning was stern.

I guessed there must be something wrong. After I had stared at her for a length of time, she relented.

"You will understand in God's good time. Now tell me, how many people of our color did you see at that church? Did you see anybody with a shit color like yours or mine? That is what those people think of us. They were all high-yellow people, were they not?" Grandma was mumbling aloud to herself.

Through the years, I had come to understand the hurt and pain color division had caused within the black community. My grandma was a God-fearing woman. She had never used profanity in my presence before. It was obvious that the odds against me were fearful and unforgiving. If in God's house, I was regarded as the least of them, it's because of my unrighteousness that was attributable to me. Additionally, it was now because of my so called *shit color*. The struggle ahead of me was almost insurmountable. It became clearer that I must truly apply myself.

Nevertheless, these are the last words I recall of my grandmother. "Edith, my child, I don't care who it is that says what. He may be colored, white, green or even yellow; you are going to be somebody. Nobody is going to put you down."

Those words were said with prophetic force, and they were the guiding force for my future regardless if it was raining, sleeting or hailing. If I ever strayed from grace, I must think of my grandmother's words. I was charged to straighten up right away if I ever wandered.

Even though I was old enough to understand many things, during this time period in my life, I did not have any idea that my family was frowned upon. I did not think that the shade of my skin mattered within our race or that it was something considered even by those in better circumstances. I cannot explain my thinking completely during those years, other than I just naturally thought, it really did not matter what shade of black you were. The fact was that you were still a person of color.

Some blacks considered themselves upper class even though they were still despised. In my opinion, this is a clear example that some people actually live a life of illusion and a complete distortion of reality. This attitude still remains far beyond me. Undoubtedly, looking aback, this kind of thinking resembles the influences of Willie Lynch's mentality and how it ultimately affected slavery.

Additionally, I was not aware that we were thought of

as a single parent family. My family or any family that was structured as mine could have been the catalyst that ignited Senator Patrick Moynihan's famous case study entitled, *The Demise of the Black Family*. Even at that stage, it began to sink in that the circumstance surrounding my birth and the reality of my humanity, as a person of African descent, was the cause of derision among some of our more privileged brothers and sisters.

These life lessons gradually affect the innocent mind of a child. It affects you as if you are suffering Chinese torture whereas they inflict small cuts continually. It eventually overwhelms a child before they reach adulthood. How and why does one's skin color have such a profound effect on their acceptance in life? Even more so, why was my skin color, a testimony of whom I was and what I was expected to become?

My grandmother was set on me beating the odds. "Edith, remember that you are somebody... always! No matter what happens to you or what is done to you, you will not give way. You must and you will behave like somebody," Grandma constantly reminded me of this. I had no idea what she was getting at, but that life lesson was sinking deep within me as I grew older.

As a child, you often bruise while playing; however, you get up because life goes on. You say to yourself that you will heal and everything will be all right. What my grandma was talking about was far beyond a simple bruise. She was sharing with me the more serious pains she had endured. In her own way, she was coding me to defend against what she was forced to defend against during her life. I was not aware this was a life lesson. Nonetheless, as I grew older, this life lesson penetrated deep into my innermost being.

Pictured left to right: father Charles, Sabrina Jerome's and mother Edith enjoying Jerome's training graduation.

From left to right: Sabrina, Jerome, mother Edith.
Bottom row: Lindaya and Larmont

Pictured back row: Lorenzo, mother Ida. Front row: Charles, Edith and Uncle Jack.
Bottom Row: Lindaya

Photo of grandma Scurry April
1964, 657 Gage Street home.

Edith, October 1963 home at
657 Gage Street-age fourteen.

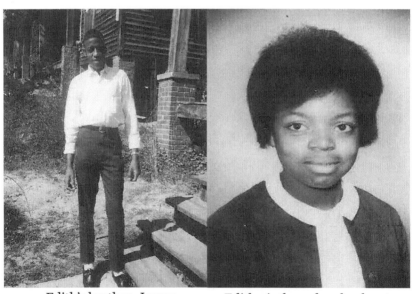

Edith's brother, James
life at 657 Gage Street 1963.

Edith ninth grade school year.

CHAPTER-THREE
Kill the Dreamer But Not the dream

My desire to become a nurse weighed heavily on me. It was all I could think about. In a dream, I once had, Nurse Robinson and Dr. Clause had decided to introduce teenagers attending Brewer High School to the inner workings of hospitals as interns. I was a young teen at the time when this opportunity offered itself. I was in the ninth grade at Brewer High School. This chance of a lifetime offered me a glimpse into the new and exciting world of hospitals and medicine.

So far, I had known Nurse Robinson at Brewer, the community nurse. She was everything. She was the only qualified black nurses that I new. There were two doctors, one white and a black doctor. The white doctor was famous within the black community. He was well-known for offering his services to Brewer Hospital instead of making loads of money at the bigger and better Self Memorial. It was once rumored that he was the butt end of jokes within the white community.

I was attracted to this program because I had seen several attractive white girls at Self Memorial. They were nicknamed Candy Stripers. Their uniforms were very nice.

Was it the pink stripes on the uniforms that made them pretty or did the hospital choose only pretty girls for the program? My mind raced with joy and the notion that I could look just like Nurse Robinson and be a real nurse like the girls at Self Memorial. I would wear a white uniform.

I was sure Nurse Robinson would introduce me to her friends as Nurse Edith Sanders. My thoughts were certainly lofty. I often dreamed of how pretty I would look. My position as a nurse would be complete with a white uniform, nurses' white cap and a huge white sash around my waist.

The girls that were to be chosen for this new exciting program had to be trail blazers. They were to prove themselves and make way for other people of color to enter into the field of medicine.

First, I would have to face that lady, Ms. Bee. It was no secret that she had her favorites. I suspect that everyone does in some way or another. I knew I certainly had special girlfriends. It was also no secret that regardless of how I was or was not treated by Ms. Bee, I would have reason to complain. Nonetheless, it never occurred to me that Ms. Bee's preferences and dislikes would run along the same distorted lines as Lydia's mother.

Here were two black women who thought identically. In Ms. Bee's eyes, I was merely a rough Negro from a rough neighborhood. In addition to me being from the wrong side of the tracks, I was also of the wrong skin color. In my family, my grandmother did not teach us indifference toward anyone.

In my dream, Self Memorial Hospital was looking for part-time workers in the dietary department. As I was approaching Ms. Bee's door, she stated, "All of the positions for the summer jobs are filled. There are no more positions," she stated bluntly while closing her door in my face. I didn't even get to put my foot inside her office. Ms. Bee was the Senior Counselor at Brewer, and next to her was Dr. Benjamin Sanders and God Almighty. I made up my mind that I was not going to be out done. When I first approached Ms. Bee's door, I did not get an opportunity to knock. She had seen me coming so she just stood in the doorway. Now her door was closed. How did she know I wanted the part-time job? I had not said anything to her about it.

I knocked, and she opened the door. She looked over the top of her eye glasses and peered down at me. Ms. Bee acted as if I was unworthy of her attention. I prayed for courage. This was going to be my first real test of courageousness. I said to myself that I am someone, and I was going to show Ms. Bee that I am somebody.

"Ms. Bee, I want to register for one of the summer jobs at Self Memorial Hospital." I said these words with as much somebody as I could summons. Ms. Bee searched me over for what seemed like an eternity.

She stated flatly, "You are not in the same class."

I knew that some of the courses I was taking were different from some of the other girls. Somehow, I was not convinced she was actually referring to my classes. I recalled her statement, "You are not in the same class." I reasoned she was not talking about the subjects we were taking. In fact, I surmised she was acting up like Lydia's mother all over again. I was that so-called person Lydia's mother had surmised my family was... those Negroes.

My grandmother was furious when I told her about what had happened. Apparently, those words were demeaning and grandma knew it. She did not try to explain anything. She simply said, "Come here Edith. Don't worry my baby. It's going to be all right." She repeated those words to herself several times as if in a trance... "it's going to be all right." Grandma wrapped her arms around me.

"That monstrous lady says you are not in her class. Ah-ha! We will show her one of these days that the dark-skinned black girl will be somebody. Then, Ms. Bee will come crawling to you for help. Edith, what goes around will someday come around. It will always end wherever it starts." Grandma Scurry kept mumbling to herself; she gave so much tongue, anger and feelings. I felt her breasts heaving when she sighed. I was darkly aware of what she was actually sharing with me. The battle for my identity and my humanity was at stake. My journey was not going to be easy. This altercation with Ms. Bee was but one small step of my journey, whereas the enemy takes no prisoners and give no quarter.

Whether I liked it or not, I was in this fight to the death. I was going to be somebody, anybody that was somebody, was who I was going to be. In my inner being, I knew grandma was going to make this happen if it was the last thing she did. But how was this going to be, neither grandma nor I knew. I guessed that in her unyielding faith, she was going to will it through her absolute faith in God.

Admittedly, Ms. Bee was somebody, and she never let you forget it. Her enemies created mishaps against her. When the mishaps occurred, everyone relished those moments when things went wrong.

It was said that Ms. Bee was so clean the black community did not visit her with the exception of the preacher. In those days, White's did not go to black folk's houses just to socialize. Therefore that channel of fellowship was closed to her. In her house a cat was not allowed. Its hairs would have messed up her fine furniture. I recall this one occasion when it was said that Ms. Bee went too far with her husband. Mr. Bee, being a carpenter, returned home in the evening after a gruesome day trying to repair a neighbor's roof. A drizzle of rain had caught him unawares, but he had to finish what he had begun, or the family would have to be moved to other shelter. He finished the job and went home late that evening. Of course, Mr. Bee was hoping for a hot cup of coffee and a warm meal. Tired and hungry, he removed his work jacket and left it on the floor in the foyer. He was too tired to remove his dirty shoes. At that instance, Ms. Bee went ballistic. There were many witnesses to confirm this.

Mr. Bee like an obedient dog, went back into the foyer, put on his warm work jacket, drove his truck to his mother's house and never returned. Thus, that ended Ms. Bee's marriage. This story was repeated countless times in whispers, and those who repeated it, showed much empathy for Mr. Bee.

People whispered, "The poor man had taken enough." It seemed that Ms. Bee cared far more for her fine things than her beloved husband. If this was true, it is a wonder Mr. Bee stayed as long as he did. After all, he was a carpenter.

This was my second time I had gone through this kind of thinking from black people. This time, however, it was affecting my ambitions and the dreams I held for my future. Several times this antiblack mind set had befallen me. I was truly bewildered as to where I could turn for help. Ms. Bee's mind was made up, and I was not allowed a day in court. There was no recourse for me. Ms. Bee and Dr. Benjamin Sanders, the revered principal of the school, were like glove and hand. They were united in their decisions and their thinking. They were a team in every sense of the word. One could say they ate from the same plate. The future that I had hoped for, in the nursing field, seemed doomed and hopeless.

Seventh grader Brewer High School.

Young woman eleventh grade.

CHAPTER-FOUR
The First Storm

I was still just a little child, but at this stage of life, I was definitely growing up. I was somewhat of a grownup girl now, somewhere between twelve and fifteen-years-old. This was the stage where my grandma no longer took time to scold me. If I trespassed in anyway, she would now call me to the side and say, "Edith, you are growing up. You should know better." That was the end of it. In the past, compared to where I was in life now, ended all of what would have been severe rebukes. I simply said, "Yes grandma."

We were renting a three-room house from a white landlord. We were still living in Pecan Orchard. During that time there had been some major developments in the housing industry. Greenwood was growing and the housing industry had a lot to do with that growth. Greenwood Mills was the largest landlord in the city. Many of their houses were built with redbrick veneer. Their remaining homes were built out of wooden panels. The wooden paneled houses were substandard homes. There wasn't any indoor plumbing in any of those houses. All of the toilets were outhouses for outdoor use only.

Greenwood County Council was advising their landlords to enclose the porches to rental properties and create indoor bathrooms. Some of the best houses would also have showers. It was modern days in old times to have those kinds of facilities... piped water. The many houses in the area created a lot of employment for area plumbers.

Our landlord "flatly" refused to convert our porch into a bathroom. It had become a law that all homes must have indoor plumping or the renter must relocate to one that was compliant with this new law. Therefore, we did not have any choice but to move. This time, we moved to 657 Gage Street. We were still located in Greenwood. This time, we were right in the heart of Greenwood and in the heart of the black community.

Our living conditions improved somewhat. We had lived in a three-room house and now we were in a house that had four rooms. For the first time in my life, I had my own bedroom, and my brothers slept in the main room.

Our new home was located within three of the largest black churches in the city. They were Morris Chapel and Tabernacle Baptist Churches and Mt. Pisgah African Methodist Episcopal (AME). Morris Chapel was the largest. Their membership was about five hundred. The second largest church was Tabernacle Baptist Church, which was next door to Morris Chapel. Morris Chapel was a big name church.

Morris Chapel was only a stone's throw from Mt. Pisgah and Tabernacle Baptist Church. People who thought they were somebody attended Mt. Pisgah. My grandma figured that it was exclusive to people of a lighter skin color. Mt. Pisgah's congregation frowned upon dark skin people like my grandmother and me.

We attended Morris Chapel. It seemed not only to have strength and comfort in numbers, but also diversity. Morris Chapel's pride lay in the fact it was the largest church within the black community. The real stuff was going on at Morris Chapel. The National Association for the Advancement of Colored People (NAACP), its surrogate, the Youth Movement and the Boy Scouts of America met there.

Brewer High School was more than a mile away. The Department of Transportation (DOT) did not fund buses to Brewer. School buses were funded for white students to ride to and from school. Brewer students on the other hand, walked to and from school every day.

During this same time, I worked on Elm Court Street for a white family cleaning their home. The job had lasted for more than a year when I quit in a huff. Every day was a miserable day because I never dreamed nor saw myself as a maid. However, this particular day was the worst one of all. It had been a miserable day because of the rain, sleet and the mud. I was learning to deal with life I thought. I found that things were soon to change.

When the white kids and their friends came home, they dropped their school bags in the foyer and ran straight down the hallway in their muddy shoes to the fireplace. I thought their father would be on my side when I asked him to correct their behavior. I said to him, "Please Sir, will you tell your daughter and her friend   to leave their muddy shoes in the foyer before going into the kitchen? If they would do this, it would save me from having to mop the floor again?" I pleaded with him.

He stepped to where I was and said that his children and their friends did not have to wipe their feet before they entered the house because that's what I was there for. At that very moment, I stood up and walked out of that house. I never looked back. I was earning about seven dollars a week on that job. Shortly thereafter, luckily, I began working as a waitress at a downtown restaurant called the Lamplight.

****

I was sixteen-years-old now. The world was turning in my head. I wanted things for myself. My grandma's health was failing. She was becoming weak and fragile. I was wrapped up into myself, and I wanted what I wanted. Therefore, I was not aware of her failing health. She was talking less every day. Of course, she was never a loud person or talkative.

Grandma was deeply serious and thoughtful in her speech. Often I recall her saying, "I have done my part. Now it is your turn to carry on the baton, Edith." As I said, my head was spinning around, and I wanted things that I did not have. I was sixteen-years-old, and I was in the eleventh grade.

What was to come after would prove to be one of the most ill-timed dilemmas I could ever encounter. Yet there I was confronted with the first major storm in my life. I was nearly blown off the face of the earth. I was pregnant. Obviously, this was too much of a burden for my grandmother to bear.

My mother suddenly reappeared in our lives. Power was slowly shifting from grandma to my mother's hand. She and her husband (not our father) began to throw their weight around. They began making decisions for me and my siblings. I was soon shipped off to Philadelphia. If I had stayed in Greenwood, it would have created a scandal. So I was sent to Philadelphia to stay with my Uncle Odell and his wife, Aunt Dorothy.

****

September 9, 1965, my six-pound five ounce baby girl, Linda was born (Jeannie). Motherhood, however, quickly overwhelmed me. Everybody said Linda was the most beautiful baby they had seen. I confess that I knew nothing about being a mother. Although I had lived with plenty of love, my grandmother had not prepared me for this role.

My mother was in South Carolina. I was alone with my baby, and the only fact I knew was my daughter and I bonded at first sight. I knew in my heart that nothing would ever separate me from my child. The storm, however, blew even more so threatening. I could have never foreseen what was in the wake for my baby and me.

I had no income to speak of, and I was ignorant at taking care of babies. I was totally dependent on my Uncle Odell, Aunt and my cousin, Jessie for my well being as well as for the needs for my baby. Although they had accepted me and vowed to help me through my self-made bad situation, I realized I had created my predicament, but now it involved them too. To make things even worse, my baby was allergic to most baby foods.

We searched for an answer to Linda's allergies. From one specialist to another, and from one hospital to another hospital, we searched for the answer. I did not have health insurance for myself or my baby. All of the expenses fell on my aunt and uncle. There is truth in this old saying, *God protects fools and babies.*

We finally found the illusive answer that we were so desperately searching for. As it turned out, Linda's fragile body was willing to accept Carnation Milk when it was mixed with corn syrup. Our search took us more than ten weeks or better. Our new found remedy helped her grow in strength and beauty. She quickly became the center of my life. However, reality does not go away.

I was still sixteen-years-old, and I did not have any means of a livelihood. Taking care of a baby was not realistic and it was virtually impossible for me without help. Jessie took me to the Department of Social Services (DSS) so that I could apply for assistance. I received a monthly check of about two-hundred-eighty-dollars ($280.00). I decided, after several months, it was time for me to return to South Carolina with baby girl, Jeannie so that I could finish school.

I packed Jeannie's and my things, and we caught the train back to South Carolina. Jeannie and I returned to Greenwood to live with my mom. My mother and her husband took us in. My stepfather handled me rough as if I was merely a wayward child. My mother did nothing to deter him. I found myself in yet another predicament. For me, my living conditions went from bad to worse.

Suddenly, my mother and stepfather announced that they were going to take my baby away from me. Together they threatened to adopt her. I was not aware, at the time, of the full scope of this dilemma. It was obvious to me that my stepfather wanted me out of his house, but he wanted to keep my baby. I grew mortified and very desperate. There was no way I was going to allow anyone to separate me from Jeannie, not even my mother and her husband. I looked around frantically trying to piece together some resemblance of reality. I had to find that one thread that would lead to a better life and out of the hell where I found myself.

CHAPTER-FIVE
The Second Storm

My mother and stepfather took me to see a lawyer. They were set on putting an end to my messy life. They were going to adopt my baby. The lawyer's office looked forbidding to me. There were books upon books everywhere. The shelves were in red mahogany and the books reached the ceiling. Mr. J.M. was not only one of the oldest lawyers in town; he was one of two lawyers in town that was friendly to blacks apart from Solicitor Townes Jones, who was running for office. The rumor was that Townes Jones was friendly because he needed the black vote. This rumor turned out to be completely false. Perhaps, let us say as he became assured in his position, he took it as a badge of honor to serve all people, including those of color without fear and favor.

The books scared me. I fully understood that I was taken there to sign papers. Those signed papers were going to be filed away in one of those books or a file somewhere. What I was supposed to sign would become part of the law forever.

I was only seventeen. What chance did I have against

all those books or the laws written in them? I strengthened myself and decided that before I signed anything, I was going to at least ask a few questions that I felt were important to me and for my baby.

The lawyer's assistant said, "Mr. J.M. is ready to see you. The papers are ready."

It was obvious that the lawyer did not have too much time for me, or my questions. He assumed, since I was with my mother and stepfather, everything had been hammered out before hand.

As a formality, he said, "You are here to sign these papers." He assumed that we were all in one accord.

"Do you understand everything?" he said turning to me. "Have all the details been explained to you, Ms. Sanders?" he asked with condescension. I began to feel that the lawyer had done this many times before and that he expected me to comply. I was only a little seventeen-year-old African-American girl who got herself pregnant. I was one of many girl's in Senator Moynihan's report. I was part of a syndrome of single parents; I am now a member of a group of lawless girls, who were part of a threat to American civilization. I was now before the system that much I understood.

"No, I have some questions," I said. This took my mother, my stepfather and the attorney by surprise.

"I am supposed to sign some papers. What does that mean for me and my daughter?" I asked. Attorney J.M. as I said before was experienced so he went straight to the point.

"If you sign these papers, Linda will no longer be your daughter. She will be adopted by the Edwards here, who have kindly offered to take the responsibility of offering her a home and some hope of a future," he said with a straight face.

My God, so that was it. Those words were harsh and they cut through my spine like a cold knife. I gathered some more courage.

"Will I still be her mother? Can I take her places like Six Flags? Can I buy her clothes or discipline her?" I asked further.

Mr. J.M. answered firmly, "No! She will no longer be your daughter, and since you will continue to live with the Edwards, she will be your sister. You will give up your parental rights to her. Do you understand?"

At this point, I felt that though he was impatient with my teenage questions and stupidity, the lawyer's training had taken over, and he wanted to be sure that all the dots and t's were in place.

"Yes! Now I understand, Sir. However, I feel that I am not in a position to do that because she is my baby.

Children are God's gifts. I will do the best I can to take care of her." I stood up and walked out of his office.

Being brave is one thing. Just walking out of that office and to where was entirely different. Another reality was now facing me. My mother did not like me. My stepfather was worse. Surprisingly, both loved my daughter very much, and they bonded with Jeannie since my return from Philadelphia. Where was I to go now? I had no income of my own. I did not know anything about paying rent, buying groceries nor did I have a car.

In 1966, I returned to Brewer High School, a much chastened girl. It dawned on me that getting my high school diploma must be the first step toward self-sufficiency. I swallowed my pride and went to face that horrible, Ms. Bee. Life was hard. The future for me and my daughter looked bleak. Later on in life, I understood that people in my circumstances are ruled out of the American dream. To the system, they are only a syndrome, referred to as subjects or case studies. Moynihan's great fear was the proliferation of the single parent black family, and he saw clearly that this family was incapable or sustaining itself without immense subsidies from government.

Despite these subsidies, families remain dissatisfied and become the bedrock of insurgency, and therefore, a threat to the American policy. I was no threat to anybody. I was seventeen, but I would be eighteen soon. I was determined to take this one step, pass my high school examination and then take the next step. Moynihan was correct, however. This class of people has issues with society. I was an angry young black woman.

After feeding Jeannie, taking her to the nursery, going to school and doing my homework, I had no time left for myself. Something had to give. I was always angry. I could not bring any friends to my home. My stepfather made it very clear that I had no home to call my own, and that I was not going to bring the streets into his righteous house. If I was late, my stepfather would lock me out of the house. I had to stay on the porch while he got up to let my brothers into the house. He would lock the doors after the boys came home, which left me out on the porch for the rest of the night.

After midnight, if it was a cold night, and I could no longer endure the cold wintry air, I walked from Taggart Street to my aunt's house on East Cambridge seeking refuge. My aunt would let me in, show me a room to sleep in, hunt down some blankets from different places and say kindly, "Edith, when will this come to an end?" At that time, there was no light at the end of the tunnel. Anger was just built up in me.

One Sunday morning, I was sitting with my mom and two siblings in the room. My stepfather had been drinking. On entering, he saw me, rushed straight at me with a pocket knife and struck me on the right side of my face. I hit him back with a Coca Cola bottle, and I kept on hitting him, hitting him and hitting him. I was out of my mind. My brothers, Bowtie and David, pulled me off him; otherwise, I would have killed him. I was yelling, "Don't you ever put your hands on me again, if you do, you will regret it the rest of your life! You have escaped this time!"

Brave words are easy, as Native Americans say, but living bravely is another whole new ball game. After all, I was living in the man's house. My mother did not say a word. If she had, she had to leave. And then there were two of my brothers as well to consider. In the meantime, my life was in shambles, a complete mess. I weighed about 128 pounds. I drank liquor but food was hard to digest. I had lost my appetite. Within one month I had lost twenty pounds. The stress was slowly killing me. I had to get away from everyone. I felt that nobody loved me. I was all alone in the world. Where will I go? The truth of the matter is that I was caught between the deep blue sea and the devil.

There was only one place I could go to and that was Philadelphia to live with my aunt. I found work at a Roman Catholic Hospital run by the Sisters of Mercy.

★★★★★★★★★★★★★★★

I returned to Greenwood for a visit. Straightaway, I went to see my friend Lydia. Her mother was beyond comforting over the loss of her daughter. Lydia was not dead; no, she was a ward of the state of South Carolina's Department of Corrections (SCDC). I guess I should have said the penitentiary.

Over the years, Lydia had become overly acquainted with prison life. She became a frequent tenant. Her mother had banked on saving Lydia from the syndrome of poverty and despair. She had intimated to Lydia that God willing, she must find herself a man (preferably of lighter skin) and then all things will be added unto them.

The story is that Lydia brought home a very black boy and her mother was unforgiving. She got pregnant. With a baby to take care of now, the African student having been rejected out of their lives, Lydia went into a life of minor crime. It started with assault, and then came what was called pilfering, afterwards an unlawful acquaintance with a forbidden leaf. Her time as a guest at the state penitentiary did not bring any penitence, nor did she learn any lawful and righteous living skills. We love each other dearly, and as I write my book, I am expecting Lydia to be released from the department of corrections.

Edith looking good. Photo taken at Uncle Jack and Aunt Thelma's home.

Edith and Charles in Atlanta, GA., waiting for the bus. Daughter, Linda and Granddaughter Lindaya returning to Kentucky.

CHAPTER-SIX
Back to Philadelphia

Returning to Philadelphia was something of an anticlimax for me. This was now my second journey there. It was comforting that my uncle and aunt always had a place for me within their family, as well as in their hearts. I had a tingling feeling that this time, I should make something of myself, if only to prove myself worthy of their love.

The first step for her and for me was that she reorganized her house so as to make a room for Jeannie and I. My two cousins had to share a room so I would have a room to myself. Other arrangements soon followed. The fact that I should work to support Jeannie and myself was not an issue; I had grown accustomed to earning some money while I was in school in Carolina. So I liked the idea, if only that would make Jeannie and me a little less dependent on my aunt.

Our neighbor called through her fence to me within a few days after my arrival. "Hey, you girl! Are you the girl from South Carolina? Where is your aunt? Your aunt asked me to look out for a job for you at the hospital. Well, I just heard through the grapevine that a girl in the kitchen is pregnant, and she cannot work there much longer. Tell your aunt the name is Benjamin Brewer. He is the supervisor in the kitchen." I was not even ready to start looking for a job. Nonetheless, I could not pass up the opportunity so I told my aunt the good news that there was a possible job for me.

Now there were two things that I did not like about our neighbor's announcement. Why did this woman have to mention the girl was pregnant? Also, was it true that the supervisor at this kitchen was Benjamin Brewer? My tormentor at Brewer school was Ms. Bee who worked for Dr. Benjamin Sanders. Why do I keep on having these coincidences? I began to fear that fate was not on my side, and that bad vibrations may have followed me to Philadelphia. I knew my grandmother was an old African. It really didn't matter that she had never been to Africa, but there were things and vibes which she said she felt in her spine. She always said it was women's intuition. My grandmother swore that if she felt something, it would happen. I do not know what I was feeling at the time, but I was very uneasy.

While I was still ruminating over these thoughts, my aunt returned from her shopping. "Come here, Edith and help me carry these bags into the house. By the way, I asked my neighbor to look out for you. Has she come back yet with a report from the hospital? They always need people, and I know that they are good employers. They are Catholic Sisters you know. The whole hospital is run by women." She volunteered this information. I, however, found this information very curious. I had never seen a hospital run by women. So these women are rich enough to build a hospital and to run one.

"Edith, do not stare at me, child. Have you ever heard of the Catholic Sisters of Mercy in your life? You must live in the boondocks in South Carolina. These sisters run a hospital for women. They do an excellent job. They have taken vows of silence so the place is as quiet as a grave. They go about their business quietly, only hearing the wind take a swipe on their white habits. You will love working for them." My aunt knew when I was preoccupied.

My curiosity was further roused. What kind of people are these who take a vow of silence? And I was not sure if I knew what a vow meant. Nonetheless, I informed my aunt her neighbor had came by, and that she had announced that there was a position at the hospital in the kitchen. I left out the details about the girl being pregnant. I also told her that she was to contact Mr. Benjamin Brewer. My aunt shook her head in an accepting manner, as she absorbed each piece of information. Aunt Dorothy acted as if this was very important intelligence.

After she had assimilated everything I said, she made a snap decision. "Go inside and dress quickly and I will take you to see Mr. Brewer. Jobs at this hospital are only opened for a few days. We must strike the iron while it is still hot. How long ago did the neighbor tell you this?"

My aunt was not listening anymore. "Hurry up, child, we must take the bus." She was now commanding me as if my life depended on it. That was my aunt. She was a decisive woman. In many ways, she reminds me of grandma. Immediately she knew what needed to be done and that was her very next step.

My Aunt Dorothy had a way with words. Coming from a stressful situation in South Carolina with my stepfather, it was such a relief and a different lifestyle. Aunt Dorothy never shouted at me. Yet she was a powerful woman in the old black tradition of strong Ashanti women. She expected to be obeyed, and I am sure she would have been surprised if for any reason I did not do as she commanded. Yet she always spoke sweetly.

"Come here, pretty one," she would say.

Now I loved to hear those words. I cannot remember having heard those words since I left my grandma's comfortable home a few years back. Life, for Aunt Dorothy seemed well ordered as if there was divine favor upon her. Whether it was the good times, the country was going through or not, as economists say, a time of steady growth in the economy that made life easy for us, I cannot say.

When Aunt Dorothy said she was going to find a job for me, all she did was say the word to a few of her friends, and within a week, there was a response. She never considered there would be a negative response. I was learning something about positive attitudes. Aunt Dorothy certainly maintained a positive attitude about life. She was so sure things were going to work out for the good of everyone that was involved. Her attitude was very different from my mother and stepfather. They always call me horrible names... especially my stepfather.

During his heavy drinking, shouting always took place when he was in that mood. Aunt Dorothy's life was well ordered. However, between her chores, she had rowdy friends, and they would crowd her kitchen table and laugh uproariously, all in good jest and form.

Aunt Dorothy explained to me how to get to the hospital. The year was 1968. I knew we were supposed to see Mr. Brewer. He was the boss in the kitchen. As we approached the entrance to Mercy Hospital, my aunt met an old acquaintance, and they began immediately to chit chat, again in their uproarious ways. I knew she had met an old friend from her school days or from the church. I stood there quietly as they talked. My aunt, realizing my situation, said sweetly, "Go on, child. You know where the kitchen is.

Go there and wait for me." I did not know the location of the kitchen. I assumed it was be on the ground floor. So I proceeded and soon enough, I saw a sign that said the cafeteria.

As I entered, I was somewhat taken aback when a rough manly voice shouted at me. "Hey girl, you must be Edith. You are coming to work, are you not? Aren't you Ms. Dorothy's neice?" Before I knew it, the words had escaped from my mouth.

"How do you know who I am?" I asked.

Mr. Brewer was an authoritative man. "You don't think your aunt would look for a job for you without telling us who you were would you? Come with me. I want you to begin right away."

So Mr. Brewer took me inside the kitchen and began to take me around and introduced me to the outfit. First he took me to the pantry, making sure that I knew how important he was.

"Child, I am the only person here with the keys to this pantry. If you want anything from here, you have to tell me, and I will get it for you. Every morning, however, I lay out whatever is needed for breakfast, and after everybody has washed up the dishes, then we go for lunch. I lay out the food for lunch at ten o'clock in the morning. Lunch closes at two in the afternoon. I only do the morning shift. Another supervisor comes in the afternoon for tea and dinner. Are you okay, child?" Mr. Brewer looked at me ever so kindly.

Mr. Brewer opened what seemed like a wall storage room where uniforms were kept in neatly folded rows. I saw some white aprons, white dresses, white caps for chefs and some blue aprons, trousers and shirts. He explained to me that at the end of the day, all uniforms were to be returned to the storage room for laundry service. Each uniform had a name tag on it, so that each worker could use only his size. Oh, that was a relief. I was beginning to think that the uniforms were interchangeable. Mr. Brewer sensed my thoughts and answered me before I could ask the question. He also sensed that I was relieved by what he had said. He was smart and very perceptive.

"Child, did you think we mix the uniforms?" he stated. He stated further, "You are perhaps size four. I wear size forty in the waste. I cannot wear your size pants, even if I wanted to. So, I will take your measurements and give it to the office. For today, you can use an apron and start work right away."

My Aunt Dorothy finally arrived huffing and puffing from laughter. "Mr. Brewer, what have you done to my child? Have you put her to work already?" my aunt asked.

"If she is going to have a job, we need her to work,"

replied Mr. Brewer.

"I was going to bring her in tomorrow. Since you need her right away, it is all right if you want her to work today," stated my aunt.

"Sweetie, it is all right with you, is it not? Mr. Brewer cannot wait. His work must be done," Aunt Dorothy followed up with me.

So this was my first day of work at Mercy Hospital in Philadelphia... the city of brotherly love.

CHAPTER-SEVEN
Forgetting Myself

Life was moving very swiftly for me. I soon forgot who I was. My cousin, JoAnn worked part-time. She also had a baby. JoAnn took my Jeannie in tow. She kept my baby for me, during my working hours, which was the whole day. I bathed Jeannie, oiled her and dressed her warmly, then I rushed her to JoAnn's house nearby. Each day I had to do this prior to going to work.

Sisters of Mercy Hospital was something else. I had grown up in the South, and of course, I was only accustomed to southern Baptist ways. Here, I had to adjust my thinking because there were no Baptist here... only the Catholics.

****

Southern Baptists are known for their loud ways. If one is in the church, or in secular life, Southern Baptists are argumentative and quarrelsome. However, later in life, I came to realize that in our small town and the county of Greenwood, with its population of about 65,000, there were more than 120 churches. This meant that per one-hundred blacks, and perhaps two hundred whites had their own church.

Life in the south goes something like this, especially in my neighborhood. The Chief Deacon picks a fight with the pastor, usually over something very minor, at least that is the way it looks in public. The real issue is always that the chief deacon feels that he has been disrespected, or bypassed in a minor decision by the pastor. He keeps it in his heart until an opportune time comes. The opportunity comes during the church's quarterly meeting and just before the annual meeting. The pastor's contract, is renewed during the third year. The rumbling starts at the beginning of the third year, just before the first quarterly meeting.

If the chief deacon fails to convince the other deacons not to renew the pastor's contract, that deacon takes his whole family away from the church and start their own church in a corner warehouse. The proliferation goes on and on forever, until there is no street corner without a Baptist church.

$$\ast\ast\ast\ast\ast\ast\ast\ast\ast\ast\ast\ast\ast\ast\ast$$

The Sisters of Mercy had taken a vow of silence, or so it seemed to me. When Mother Superior visited, she walked around the kitchen with Mr. Brewer. As far as I could see, she said nothing. She carried a note pad to record on during her visits. To my surprise, as she approached me, she knew me by name. I realized later that she was a quick reader. I was wearing my name tag. Although she said very little, she touched me and said, "God bless you, my child." This was surprising because she said the same words to grown men as well. Otherwise, she nodded in an acknowledging way as she went to our various stations. Of course we stood frozen to our positions in clean white uniforms because we were always told in advance when she was coming. Very often she touched everyone on the shoulder kindly, but said nothing. At other times she made a sign of the cross and then went on.

Still even more surprising, if the kitchen was clean, Sister Superior went out quietly. She said nothing to Mr. Brewer. Of course, he exhaled with a sigh of relief. He smiled saying, "The Mother Superior is pleased.

One day, when I got the courage, I asked, "Mr. Brewer, how do you know she is pleased, if she says nothing?"

"Child, if Mother Superior is not pleased you will know it," Mr. Brewer replied. "Her face becomes frozen. She hates any form of uncleanness, which she associates with the devil. She will stop by the large cooker and take up the scrapper or wire brush; then we know we are in trouble. With her established customs, I know when I am in trouble," he continued.

During the time I worked at the hospital, I never saw Mother Superior touch any of the washing utensils that Mr. Brewer described in that dreadful and fearful way. I remember Dr. Benjamin Sanders cordially speaking with students at Brewer High School. He stood at the school entrance and told those students, who came after the bell rang, to go home. Come to think of it, I do not remember Dr. Sanders actually saying anything to the kids that were late. It was understood that if the bell rang and Dr. Sanders stood at the gate, no one could enter.

I realize that a well-ran establishment, like that of the Sisters of Mercy Hospital, had very clear guidelines of expectations. The guidelines and expectations were apparently understood by everyone that worked there. The mark of a good establishment is that their guidelines are self-enforcing. I did what I was told and I obeyed all the rules. The rules of engagement were understood by everybody. This was also the case at Brewer High School. It was the threat, rather than the actual enforcement of rules by the Mother Superior that forced us to freeze in our position as she passed on her inspection tours. Life is amazing.

Mildred was renting her own pad. She had it decorated very nicely. I dreamed, I will have my own pad one day. When this materialized, I was going to decorate my pad the same way Mildred had done hers. She was immediately my heroine.

Mildred knew the city just like the palm of her hand. She would say, "Catch bus 121 at 7.00pm." From my aunt's house, the bus takes thirty minutes to the next exchange. From there I would catch bus 140. It dropped me off at Liberty Street... one block from the Eagle Club.

I had never gone to a club in Greenwood. This was all new to me. It was even more fascinating that Jesse knew her way around. She also knew the people there. Jesse knew about the drinks on the shelf by name and which drink to buy. She knew about Johnny Walker, Teachers, Jamaican Rum, Trinidadian Rum, Russian Vodka and even Bavarian beers.

Bavarian beers, she told me, are best served when warm. Since the bartender served them cold, it was supposedly no good. I, however, settled on Jamaican Rum. Rum was soothing, it was mildly sweet and tingly in my throat as it went down. As it settled in my stomach, I experienced a sense of serenity and peace. Jamaican Rum offered me that feeling that surpasses all understanding. I tried other drinks, of course, such as beers, particularly the German beers because they were very popular. I eventually settled on Jamaican Rum. My life was good at age nineteen.

CHAPTER-EIGHT
The Prodigal Daughter

I loved life in Philadelphia. Jesse and I became really hot friends. Jesse was always the life of the party. Christmas time was always a roaring time of fun and pleasure for us. On this one particular Saturday, word was out that the Cotton Club was going to treat all "ladies" to a shindig in anticipation of Christmas. Beer and mixed drinks were flowing freely, therefore, we could drink as much as we liked. Boys were dressed in fantastic costumes for Christmas. There was one guy who was dressed as Santa Claus. There were no charges to ladies. I said the drinks were on the house.

I was totally green to the ways of the city. Unknown to us, the guys would pay the owner for the privilege. They had persuaded the owner of the club to make this offer. Jesse liked a challenge. She was daring and bold. At other times her boldness surprised me but that was Jesse. On this night, her first drink was Scotch. I said, "Jesse, take your time the night is early. It is only 10pm. The club is open until 1am." She ignored me. The drinks were free. In a short time she had another Scotch.

If a customer got drunk, the club owner asked them to go outside and sober up. I would have been really lost as how to treat this situation, if Jesse had to do this. I was not familiar with anyone there so I wanted her to tread water lightly. The night had just begun, and she was downing her drinks as if she was drinking water.

Santa Claus was supposed to drop by the Club at midnight. The club owner announced the final call for drinks soon afterwards. Attendees would stock up at this time, ordering several beers or drinks of hard liquor. Some guy, named DeMario asked, "Do you want anything?" I said no.

I further stated, "I have already had several rums." I was standing near the dance floor when everyone rushed to get the last drink for the night. It was always the custom that after 12:00 midnight the dancing got heavy and almost everyone was on their feet. As people were dancing, they would at intervals stop by their table to take a long sip of whatever they were drinking.

I went to the bathroom, leaving two guys at our table. While I was away, the lights were turned off temporarily. Like a blind person, I slowly felt my way back to my seat. Slowly, the club owner lit candles so that we could at least see. Apparently this was not the first time this had happened because the club owner seemed prepared. Neon lights and flashing signs started flashing over the dimly lit floor.

The neon lights distorted whatever small light there was. I could hardly see beyond the dance floor. I looked for Jesse. She was not on the dance floor; at first I thought she was in the bathroom; but I had just come from there. I went back into the bathroom to look again. There was no Jesse. Suddenly the ceiling lights came on. I immediately went into panic mode since she was not on the dance floor. I did not see her anywhere.

I went to the entrance door of the club to look for her. Jesse was wearing a long white dress, rather than the red which was popular during Christmas time. She felt that Christmas should really be associated with snow, therefore, she wore white.

As I continued my search outside, I saw a woman was being lifted into the back seat of a car. A piece of white cloth was hanging out of the car door. Suddenly, it struck me like a bolt of lightning! Jesse was the only one wearing white tonight. Assuredly, Jesse would not leave without letting me know that she was going and what I should do.

I heard DeMario shouting to some other guys, "Quick guys, put her in the car before that stupid niece of hers comes out of the club. She refused to drink any of our stuff!"

My responses were not motivated by any sense or rhyme, just sheer panic. I guessed that what DeMario had given Jesse to drink was intended to have an overpowering effect on both of us. I cried out frantically for help. "Help me! Help me! Someone, please help me!" Straightaway, the parking lot was flooded with cars turning on their lights.

The club owner ran outside toward me. "What is wrong, lady?"

I told him, "Something is up with DeMario and those guys with him. They are trying to abduct my cousin, Jesse." What I did and said was apparently enough to cause a real commotion. One thing club owners disliked was drawing unwanted attention from the police.

The club owner and I found Jesse lying on the back seat of DeMario's car in a drunken stupor.

The club owner asked DeMario, "Who is that lady on the backseat of your car?" DeMario didn't even know Jesse's name.

"It is my cousin, Jesse!" I shouted. "They are trying to abduct my cousin!" My ranting must have done it.

"Get that girl out of your car right now or I will call the cops!" shouted the club owner.

"Ms., I will call a taxi for you. Just tell me where you live. I will take care of the fare," the owner said.

I was so terrified all I could do was nod. I am uncertain if I made sense or not, I really do not remember.

The club owner was very nice and caring. He paid for the cab and directed it to where we were going from my questionable directions. I sat in the back of the cab with Jesse crying hysterically. She lay there still in a drunken stupor. It was now well past 1am. I thank God for that club owner's generosity and help. I did not have any money to pay the cab driver. When we arrived home, I ran into the house to search for some cash. I left Jesse in the taxi. I wanted to give the driver a small tip. In the city, it was customary to leave a tip. He had been nice to us also. He had taken us straight to our house just as the club owner told him. I guess that I made enough sense to him even though I do not recall anything I said to him.

I made so much noise my aunt woke up.

I rushed back to the car to get Jesse. She staggered in slowly still drunk from whatever those guys had given her to drink.

I remember that Jesse was sitting at the kitchen table sipping a cup of hot coffee like a prodigal daughter that had been brought back from hell. I asked Auntie Dorothy to pour some coffee for me as well. This was unusual. I never asked my auntie to do anything for me. It would have been disrespectful. She told me the next day I looked like a ghost. Being a true African

American, I must have gone through something really shocking for my face to appear pale and ghostly looking. I was scared and frightened. Jesse had never gotten drunk before from drinking. She would become noisy, but that was all.

I began to wonder if there was a link between the free drinks and DeMario's secret plan. Whoever tripped the lights must have been part of the scheme also, which gave DeMario and his friends enough time to abduct Jesse. Jesse had never gotten drunk on me before when we were out drinking. I began wondering what was in that Scotch Whiskey she drank. I clearly recall that Demario and his friends kept offering me some of the same bottle but I was drinking Rum. Question after question kept popping up in my mind flooding through my little brain. But through it all, I said nothing to my aunt.

My aunt was well schooled in the ways of the world. She knew something had happened which turned out badly. She was nursing Jesse. Standing behind her, she caressed her back slowly as if singing a lullaby to a child. She said nothing for a long time. I nursed my cup of coffee, sipping little drops of it at a time as if fearful that the cup would run dry. My aunt never shouted or raised her voice. She was used to being obeyed. She turned slowly in my direction. "Girls, there must be something terribly wrong about the way you are living your lives. God does not like it," calmly my aunt said.

She said it so slowly, so calmly, almost like a whisper. We sat there for about another hour or longer as Aunt Dorothy brought another cup of coffee to Jesse. I dared not steer out of my chair. I was almost afraid that if I moved, I would provoke the wrath of God. Until my aunt gave us permission to leave the table, I would not leave. In any case, I had to stay because my aunt might decide to ask questions about what we had done.

The lesson she wanted to teach us was that God did not like the way we were living our lives. In a very serious way, I pondered what was I to do now? I had to answer this bewildering question, and I felt that I did not have a lot of time to get the answer.

CHAPTER-NINE
Prodigal Daughter's Revelation

More than thirty years have passed since that day and my revelation has become clearer with each passing day. It goes back three-hundred-years, when black women took the responsibility of saving the race from slave owners. They used certain words repeatedly in a way we can only describe as coded language. My grandmother had used the phrase, "Edith, you are going to be somebody. Even if you are not somebody, you are going to carry yourself as if you are somebody."

Now, in my mature years, I know and can ascertain a child who has been brought up according to the strict African American tradition. Poverty was no excuse. That did not make you a beggar. Lack of formal education was no excuse. That did not make one an ignoramus. My grandmother could barely read or write. Her one piece of literature was the Bible. Even at that she sometimes asked me to read certain passages for her. It was from that book of wisdom that she gathered all her mastery of the world. She had a peculiar view of the world.

As I sat with my aunt, sipping my coffee, assimilating her words of wisdom, I understood and knew that my destiny was much larger than a dish washer in the hospital kitchen with the Sisters of Mercy. Although the Sisters had been kind, compassionate and willing to dignify my work, I recognized that if I tarried longer, I would never rise beyond this station. I would never be somebody. I would never be able to say, like the Centurion in the Bible, *to this one, come and he cometh, to the other go, and he goeth.*

I still loved to party, and my friends say that I am a show off. I am the life of any party. I like clothes, and I like good things, but clothes and good things must be dignified with some achievement by the one who wears them.

Three weeks later, I went to Mr. Benjamin Brewer and gave my notice. I thanked him kindly, and said, "I am going back home to resume my schooling. A new nursing school has opened back home. The Vocational School is recruiting students. My brother is working in the kitchen at Self Memorial Hospital. He will start the process for me before I arrive."

There is an advantage in writing one's biography in the after years of one's maturity. I can now see some divine intervention in the events that followed. The school wanted one more student in order to make their minimum number required to justify the need. All was now set for a new chapter in my life. So, when I arrived in Greenwood, I was told to report to the Director of the Nursing School without further delay.

I started school right away that fall. My church life was predetermined by my grandmother. Reverend Dr. Ed Johnson had just taken over the ministry at Morris Chapel in Greenwood. He was young, chubby but handsome and very political. The year was 1973, and the times were aflame with change. Morris Chapel was the center of social and political activity. There was the Young People's Wing of the National Association for the Advancement of Colored Peoples. Ms. Bee was its director. There was a youth choir and other organizations for young people. Dr. Johnson associated himself with the Little River Missionary Association. He was also a friend of the new president of Lander College, a college newly adopted by the state of South Carolina.

I have mentioned these details to say that any young man or woman who wanted some action or association with his peers was likely to find his niche somewhere in this matrix.

I remember very well when I first met Charles. He was twenty-six-years-old and as straight as a ram rod. Clean shaven, straight out of the US Army. Charles spoke softly, gentle in his movements but very manly with his grip. He set my heart on fire. A few days later, he came to visit me at my apartment.

I was playing with my daughter, Jeannie. Charles was attracted to Jeanie right away. Jeannie has a magic way of attracting people, and she easily bonded with them. My stepfather was everything I hated in a man, but Charles was everything I needed. He was as gentle as a lamb with Jeannie.

So, I loved Charles. We bonded right away. I knew in my heart, as only a woman can know, this man is the one. But, having been hurt before, I wanted to make sure that he was Mr. Right. Eighteen months passed before we were officially able to tie the note. I was hooked for life. Charles complimented me in every way. I was bubbly, vivacious and adventurous, it was Charles however, who kept the ship away from the storms. It was to Charles I came back to after a stormy day and I wanted a hug and comfort and a harbor away from the storms of life. Charles says very little. He listens while I talk until I fall asleep.

My studies went smoothly. Presumably, there's a difference between a child and a mature adult going to school. If I did not understand something, my first plea for support was my study group. Often, we met at my house. They were surprised that each time we met, we had to go over questions and materials I had set aside for discussion because I did not understand something. This always occurred before we dealt with any new material. My apartment quickly became the group's study room. Charles as usual, was content as could be, taking Jeannie away from our studies, feeding her or singing to her a lullaby. He was quite methodical.

Charles bought Jeannie children's books and read them to her. I became jealous as Jeannie grew fond of Charles. Each time Charles came home, Jeannie left me and ran to Charles. Hours would pass before I saw either of them. Most days, when Charles and Jeannie were off playing, it was only until I announced that dinner was ready that I would see them again.

CHAPTER-TEN
The Time in Between

Working at Self Memorial Hospital at one time brought joy, and at other times, it brought excruciating pain. Sometime in 1968, Greenwood County was given a choice, they either close Brewer Hospital, or begin taking both blacks and whites at Self Memorial Hospital. This move, actually marked the beginning of integration.

Self Memorial Hospital was named after one of the Self's, the leading industrialists in Greenwood County. The Self family, by all accounts, was benevolent patriarchs. It would behoove anybody who wanted to go anywhere and to be somebody in Greenwood County, to be at peace with the Self's. There are many legends told about their generosity and their propensity to protect the weak. These stories usually refer to Papa Self, sometimes known as Big Jim Self.

Big Jim employed a black butler, a maid and an errand boy. The story is that when the winds of change in racial affairs came, at the time of the death of Dr. Martin Luther King in 1968, Papa Self decided to go along with it, rather than be caught by the tail winds of change. His decision was intended to make a lot of difference to Greenwood County, and to make its race relations, the envy of the neighboring counties.

The story is that many white folks had not seen the coming changes. One of them was a store renter in one of the Greenwood Mills villages. The Butler had been sent on an errand, and he was kept waiting at the corner store because a group of white folks just hanging out there kept the store keeper chatting away time. Papa Jim wanted to know why the Butler was late.

The Butler told his story. It appears that the store-keeper verified the story to the effect that he thought the Butler was just one of those Negroes and he wasn't going to be bothered with. To cut a long story short, the store-keeper's lease was not renewed.

The hospital was the newest hospital in all of the five counties surrounding Greenwood county. It was the pride of the Greenwood. Black nurses were hired. One Wilma Hughes, a registered nurse and a Greenwood native, who had gone to Philadelphia but returned home, was the only black supervisor for years.

Relationships between patients and black nurses took a turn for the worse, especially with those folks not yet used to seeing blacks in responsible positions. I would go into a room, turn the patient to make sure they were comfortable and administer medications. This white female patient turned around and said, "Maid, when is my nurse coming?" I answered and said, "Madame, I am the nurse." A sigh of disappointment showed on her face.

In an atmosphere where the patient is king, any complaint by a white patient was taken seriously, as it should have been, but I felt that they were exaggerated. This led to many losses of black nurses migrating to metropolitan hospitals, which they thought were more accommodating to diversity.

It was also my disappointment that in thirty-years of service, I can remember only two black nurses who achieved the rank of supervisor. I feel that more could have been done. Human relations take time to coalesce, and I feel that the new generation will have fewer problems than we did.

At that time, my social activities centered on my three children, my husband, and my church Morris Chapel Baptist Church. However, without warning, I was drawn into the mainstream of local politics in 1990. The School Board's elections were held on an at large basis. Since the black population constituted only 31 percent of the population, the odds were stacked against people of color ever making it to the board.

There were issues in the school system which needed addressing. The ratio between black teachers and white teachers needed to be addressed. We did not have sufficient representation at the administrative head office to make an impact on black life. Even more worrying, the system reflected the prejudices of the wider community, making structural racism significant in the disproportionate numbers of black kids on punishment. We were also losing black teachers on a yearly basis. As the veterans retired from Brewer and other former black schools, new opportunities for black kids opened in the wider economy, fewer and fewer blacks applied for teaching positions.

My children were now in middle school. We were losing role models for our kids. Sure there were many white teachers who were wonderful with black kids, but we felt that there was a need to keep some black role models in the school district. Morris Chapel was the hub of all these discussions. We were soon joined by Donald Robinson and Reverend Willie Harrison. Robinson and Reverend Harrison brought Methodist Reverend DeQuincy Newman to a *POW WOW* at Trinity Methodist Church. That *POW WOW* was the mother to the formation of the NAACP in Greenwood.

I was merely a concerned citizen and was minding my own business and the business of raising my children. Somehow, whether it was Dr. Johnson, Dr. Harrison or Robinson, I do not know. They found that my gift lay in organizing people and inspiring a crowd to action. We sued Greenwood School District in Federal

Court. The issue, to us, was clear cut. Their at large electoral system was designed to disfranchise blacks. Single member districts were formed on the school board, city and County Council.

This foursome were towering figures to me. The foursome worked like this. Dr. Johnson was the heart. His personality was full with the love of Jesus Christ, and he would minister to folks beyond his church. Dr. Harrison and James Wakefield were the thinkers and strategists while Councilman Robinson was the mouth. Robinson was absolutely fearless. Our agenda in those days was to speak out for black folks and advance the cause of equal treatment. Looking back now, we fell far short of Dr. Martin Luther King's dream, to love all men. Little did I know then that these four and Dr. Newman before them were pioneers, and that later on, I would wear Elijah's mantle.

During the late 80's until the early 90's, the city of Greenwood decided they would cut a road through our neighborhood instead of from bypass 72 NE. It was as if we had no say so in their decision. Not so, this was our neighborhood. We were not going to take this lying down. New Market Park sued the city. The case was won with the assistance of Mayor John Nave and Senator Strom Thurmond. As it turned out, the city of Greenwood found the money to build the entrance road from bypass 72.

The vision grew slowly. Although I represented a black district on the County Council, there were many white folks who lived there. They had concerns too. If I took these concerns seriously, they wanted their streets lighted, they abhorred crime, they wanted a recreational area for after school play and events; these were human concerns outside the boundary of race. I became a transitional leader for my district. I became a friend for all the people, black and white. I must emphasize that this reality came slowly, and that I did not seek it aggressively at the time.

Greenwood's political machine works along a familiar path. Once the invisible leadership decides that certain customs and usages have served their time, rather than fight the birth of new customs and usages, they prepare for a new birth and thus pre-empt violent disruption of society.

I was, therefore, surprised by the speed with which the school board adopted the new single district electoral system in 1994 and introduced a system of rolling off so as to keep some continuity on the board. I ran for the board in 1994, being one of 12 vying for three seats. I won a seat in 94 and 98. In 2000, I ran without opposition. The electoral system then changed from a two-year term to a four-year-term.

CHAPTER-ELEVEN
Nurse Edith-LPN II
A Testimony by Janie Bryant

Nurse Edith was always adorned with a crisp white hand-pressed dress, white no-run support hose, white non scuffed nursing shoes, a good ticking Timex watch and that hard-earned white nursing cap and pin. Fully dressed, she headed off to work every day at the local county hospital. Edith maintained the attitude of looking forward to a good day and prayed that all went well.

Edith's daily motto was *I can and I will make a difference in the lives of others.* Scripture held her to this belief:

But it shall not be so among you: but whosoever will be great among you, let him be your minister; And whosoever will be chief among you, let him be your servant: Even as the Son of man came not to be ministered unto, but to minister, and to give his life a ransom for many (Matt 20:26-28 (KJV).

Mrs. Childs viewed nursing as a call to serve those in need. For more than thirty-two-years, she dedicated herself to delivering the best quality nursing care she could. Everyday was different, interesting and very challenging. All the same, Edith left work feeling confident that she had given her best to all she had cared for during her shift.

She felt it is not just her duty but a right that each patient was treated with the utmost care, respect and dignity. As she put, "That is what we all should want from anybody." To provide these various acts, Edith possessed these qualities:

A caring nature-it mattered how one was feeling, hurting or needing her to respond. Edith was able to perform her duties, and she was accountable for all she did. "You gonna do it, mean it, don't do it, because if your hearts not in it, it won't work," she was known to proclaim.

Edith was very attentive to her patient needs. She took time to do the little things that meant most to her patients, like giving a soothing back rub, changing the bed linens three to four times after an accident with a bedpan and listening to the countless problems of a patient. Through all of that Edith still held the hand to comfort her patients. In addition to her nursing care of patients on the job and others in the community, Edith has given personal and intimate care to members of her own family. This does not include the hours of care and support she has so often provided to individuals and friends in the community that needed assistance during their sicknesses or rehabilitative stages. Her nursing acts were continuous. To Edith "a patient was a patient" she did not discriminate. When they needed cleaning, changing or care Edith stepped in with the caring touch she was known for.

In many ways, some patients received their healing through excellent care. Edith was a well-respected nurse and role-model to student nurses assigned to her precept.

Nurses care for people who are both ill and healthy, no matter of age, culture or demographics. This also included attending the physical and emotional, psychological and social needs as well as the spiritual needs of a person. Edith (Nurse Childs) has had numerous experiences in meeting these kinds of needs for her patients.

As a surgical nurse, Edith recalls the hopes and joys of witnessing the amazing recovery of a patient. Many were diagnosed with debilitating illnesses but regained their health and returned home. She felt that some of her most difficult care was often given to the patients that were beyond the reaches of medical care. This is where Nurse Childs recalls moments spent consoling grieving patients and their families. She ensured a quiet and peaceful atmosphere which ended in a dignity.

Edith is involved in her community as an advocate for

health and wellness. She introduced Health Ministry Nursing to her church congregation and community. These programs promote healthy living and lifestyles, disease prevention and other educational clinics.

After reporting to work, clocking in and out, during days of chaos, overtime, lost lunch-breaks, patient overloads, low-staffing, code blues, call backs, shift fights, policy changes, hospital renovations, dealing with the new hires and retirees, it was time for me to say, "I came, I did, I served and now it is time to retire from the hospital that was once segregated, whereas blacks were not allowed admission or unit employment."

With Edith's retirement came moments of joy and excitement. And from the medical field it was time to realize and reflect on her years of service that would never be replaced. Edith hailed from a breed that became nurses because they loved it. It was not for the money.

There exists a nursing shortage in part because nurses today are not dedicated to the profession as the ones of nurse Edith's time. Again Edith says, "If you are gonna do it, do it right the first time."

Although Edith has retired, she continues to apply her knowledge and skills in support of others. "Nursing will always be in my blood," she smiles.

A NURSE'S PLEA
Janie Bryant

Lord guide me along the way
As I journey onto work today
Guide my hands as I give care
To all those in need
Help me Lord to do my best
To honor and uphold the nursing creed.

Guide my mind to always be alert, focused and hear
Help me to be attentive to all I see think and hear.
Guide my steps as I go
From room to room and hall to hall.
Let me be prompt to answer
Each patient's wanting call

Guide my heart to be loving, caring, kind and true
Let me be a shining example
and expression of you
Guide me daily with enduring courage, strength and hope
When faced with trials and challenges
Please help me to cope.

Guide me dear Lord
For each day is just another test
Help me to stand tall, to stay strong
And always do my very best
Let me feel fulfilled and gratified
At the day's long end
Prepared, refreshed and ready
To start it all over again.

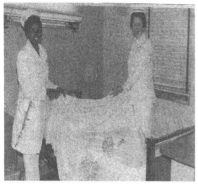

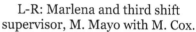

L-R: Marlena and third shift supervisor, M. Mayo with M. Cox.

Pictured is Head Nurse, Inez Kennemore and Edith preparing bed for patient admission.

Photo of Little River Baptist Association Health Care Ministry(LRBAHCM). L-R: Edith, (health care coordinator), Ojetta Williams, (assistant coordinator), and Louise Walker. Back row-L-R: Charles Childs, Nancy Cole, Gregory Logan, Geneva Thomas (secretary), Stephanie Patton and Alfonso Davis.

Pictured is Percilla Anderson (CNA) and Edith Childs, Ministry of Health nurse at Morris Chapel Baptist Church.

CHAPTER-TWELVE
More Storms in My Life
1975 My Life Really Changes

February 1975, I was admitted to Self Memorial Hospital with blood clots in my left leg. I did not want to be there, but the Lord needed to slow me down to guide me into getting my act together. Dr. Holloway placed me on complete bed rest, and I was not to get up for any reason. I had no excuse because I am to blame for my health issues. I never thought that I would end up in this mental or physical state. I was simply exhausted.

I asked the doctor to give me something to calm me down. He prescribed Valium at three doses a day. The Valium induced a drowsy state in me. Therefore, I was unable to keep my eyes open. About 10pm that afternoon, I slipped into a deep sleep. As I was sleeping, I felt something pulling me backwards and into a large black hole. In the black hole, there were no stars or light of any kind. There was only darkness.

In my mind, I knew without a doubt, I was on my way to netherworld. I was the only one traveling through this black hole. Although I tried desperately to speak, I was unable to utter a word. I struggled silently as I was drawn into this dark vortex.

The blackout lasted the entire night. It was about 7am the next morning, when my friend, Emma Morton, who worked on the same floor with me came in. Emma and I had started our nursing careers together as nursing assistants. When she found me, I was fully sedated. My blood pressure was very low and she recorded a very slow heart beat. Certainly, I was on my way to Hades. Emma called for the head nurse to come in to check me out. The head nurse came first, and following her were a host of other nurses, technicians and doctors.

I could hear the medical staff talking among themselves about what to do next. They asked me a series of questions. I tried to respond but I do not recall saying anything. I was moved closer to the nurses' station for precautionary measures. This was done to ensure a quick response if another episode occurred like the one that caused me to be there in the first place. They were monitoring me very closely.

My doctors stopped all of the recent prescriptions I had been given. Within forty-eight hours I was feeling a lot better, however, I required assistance walking. Although my blood pressure was still up somewhat, I was released from the hospital after three more days of observation.

****

August 14, 1975 approximately 2:30pm, I attended the Reverend Ernest Angle Conference, which was held at Greenville Memorial Auditorium. Reverend Angle asked, "Will the attendees, who want to give their life to the Lord Jesus Christ, come forth."

As I sat there reflecting on every word of his sermon, his words jumped out at me as if his sermon was written for me. I had heard other people saying that it seemed that the preacher was talking to them.

He said in an authoritative but inviting voice, "Are you tired of living the way you have been living? Then this invitation is just for you. Today is your day! Come to the altar right now and give your heart to the Lord. Ask Him to come into your life and forgive you all your sins."

I did not look around to see who was getting up. All that I knew was that I had to make it to the altar. I was compelled by what I will gladly say was the Lord Almighty. I did finally look around, and I found that I was not the only one. Many other people had made the decision to come to the altar that day.

I asked the Lord Jesus Christ, "Lord, come into my heart and into my life."

I recited the sinner's prayer because I believed that God had sent His son to live amongst men for thirty-three-years. And that He died for my sins just so I could have the right to eternal life. I accepted Jesus into my life that afternoon. I was freed from judgment and conviction.

All that I can remember is trying to maintain my composure and keep myself from falling. No matter how hard I tried to stop my fall, I kept falling. I heard my head echoing when I hit the cement floor, yet I felt no pain from my fall. When I came around, I felt physically lighter as if all of my burdens, my cares and concerns had been lifted away from me. I felt like a new person, and that I was actually going through life for the very first time... but everything was familiar and purer.

The Lord has blessed me tremendously since that August day. One may ask, "Have you sinned since that day?" The answer is, "Yes, I have sinned, but I know my Lord is forgiving. When He forgives, He forgets."

At times, God has revealed things to me before they happen. When it came to pass, it was just the way God had revealed it. He showed me that some of my family members would spend time in prison. Some have and some still are.

In 1977, God revealed that I would become pregnant again and this time with a son. He would be healthy, handsome and intelligent. May 4, 1977, I gave birth to a son that was healthy, he is handsome and very smart.

In 1997, our son, Larmont was stabbed in his stomach, while he was trying to help someone else. He nearly died that night. Larmont received medical attention from the local hospital in the area where he was attending school. He was sent back to his dorm to rest for the remainder of the night. As a parent feeling uneasy and very concerned, I wanted to see my child for myself. Therefore, at about 11pm that night, Charles and I packed up to go see about our child. Because we were not satisfied with the way we found Larmont, we drove him to Self Memorial Hospital in Greenwood, South Carolina.

Dr. E. Rapp was the attending physician that night. He came to the ER, took one look at Larmont and ordered x-rays. From the x-rays, Dr. Rapp saw that Larmont was bleeding internally. He stated that one dreaded word, *Surgery*! He said that Larmont had a lacerated liver and needed to be prepared for laparotomy surgery. Dr. Rapp's diagnosis was that Larmont had an abdomen full of blood.

As Charles and I waited patiently, we prayed that God would have His way in this situation, and that He would guide Dr. Rapp's hands. We also prayed that God would hold on to Larmont through surgery. God was already healing Larmont. Dr. Rapp found a blood clot on Larmont's liver. This clot had stopped the bleeding. "I have reviewed the x-rays further, the clot revealed that Larmont's surgery was successful."

"My God," was all I could think or say. The Bible says, *Confess your faults one to another, and pray one for another, that ye may be healed. The effectual fervent prayer of a righteous man availeth much (James 5:16 (KJV).*

We saw firsthand what prayer can do. Larmont was discharged that following Thursday afternoon, and he returned to school several weeks later. The following Friday, Charles was diagnosed with cancer. This time we were girded and protected by prayer and supplication. We weathered the storm.

*Pray without ceasing (*1 Thess 5:17 (KJV). We did just that! Charles' surgery went well. Dr. Mulkey was his surgeon, and he was able to remove all of the cancer. Until this day, he is cancer free. Charles was due to be discharged in seven days, however, he was doing so well, they released him in five. Glory be to God, because God had shown Himself as our source of power. God had shown up and showed out.

In 1998, Charles' third brother was diagnosed with cancer, and in 2004, his fourth brother was also diagnosed with cancer. As of today, Charles and his brothers are doing well. All that we say or do is give thanks daily for these blessings. If we looked solely at statistics, these four brothers were not supposed to beat the odds, but my God said, "No!"

John brings another pan for chicken during free Christmas dinner.

Charles and Edith while in Japan poses in front of a jewelry store.

Wilhelemia Robinson, Edith (not pictured Dr. Robert Moore-co-authors) shares the cover of the *Brewer More Than A School* during Alumni Banquet.

Nancy Walker and Sara Ouzts serving healthy snack at the Morris Chapel Health Fair.

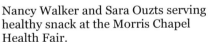

L-R bottom row: Effie White and Marie Jefferson Back row L-R: Patrica Yeldell, James Martin, Charles and Edith. Hidden behind Edith is Tommy Childs.

Council Woman Edith S. Childs and Charles pictured together as she accepts the oath of office.

L-R: Mary Green, Barbara Martin, Donald Yeldell, Pat Yeldell James Martin and Effie White.

L-R: Charles and sister Marie. Back row L-R: Edith and brother-in-law Tommy Childs.

L-R: Galen Lukie, Edith and Keta Lukie (Clerk to Council).

Edith stands by the flags that she truly honors.

The Childs family-Jerome, Sabrina and Jordan-with pet-Jasper.

L-R: The Brown family-Lorenzo and Lorenzo, II. T-R: Lindaya, Linda and Lakeyia.

Charles and Edith celebrates the Woman of Wisdom 2011.

L-R: Nathaniel and cousin, Charles, Tommy, Charles and John.

Larmont Childs' sons, Cameron and Kejuan

L-R: Council members-Mark Allison, Childs, Chair Robbie Templeton, Back row L-R: Gonza Bryant and Patrick Moody

L-R: Lisa White County Treasurer, Vic Carpenter former County Manager, Back L-R: Council Members-Chuck Motes, Childs, Vice Chair Bob Jennings and County Attorney Chuck Watson

L-R: Judge Bart McGuire after swearing in Edith Childs, Charles offers a little kiss.

L-R: Effie White, Marie Jefferson, and Sandra Hall. Back L-R: Pat Yeldell, James Martin, Edith, Tommy Childs and Larry Wise.

Edith stands for a pose.

2006 swearing in celebration .

Edith and Uncle Jack.

Senator Barack Obama and Edith strikes out with a few steps while being *Fired Up Ready to Go.*

Edith and Post 224 Commander Thomas Gaskin.

Edith and the first black Mayor Johnny Waller of Calhoun Falls, SC.

Larmont Childs posing at senior prom 1995.

Edith poses with Sellars the youngest member of SC House of Representatives while at the White House.

Childs family visiting Japan-2004.

Celebrating Mama's eightieth birthday.
L-R: Aunt Linda, Mom.
Back row L-R: Ann, David, Nathan,
Edith and James.

Charles, Lindaya, Edith and Uncle Jack.
Back Row L-R Lorenzo Brown, and Mom
pause for a quick camera shot.

Grandma Childs with Larmont
and Charles.

At the SOCO Banquet, Larmont Childs
introduces speaker, Mr. Chuck Graves.

Relatives posing after Nephew Anthony
Sanders' sermon at Mt. Tabor.

CHAPTER-THIRTEEN
Tragedy Strikes

If it were not for my husband, Charles, I would have collapsed under the weight of my responsibilities a long time ago. I had virtually given up being a housewife by 1994 when I was elected to the County Council. Charles organized the family games, the food and the outings. I joined them when I could, and when I was off the weekend, I tried to throw my weight around as the mother of my family. I think nobody in my family was taken by my pretenses.

I have said this to explain how I survived the most excruciating and painful experience of my life. My mother was aging, and I knew that I had to take care of her. Who am I to do unto others what they have done to me? My Bible says to owe no one anything but love. The responsibility for looking after her fell on me. At this time my grandmother was also in her twilight years. She also needed care.

I am told that this traditional thinking came from Africa. Even though the men provide, from time to time, among the Ashanti in West Africa, from which I came, the women take the lead in the daily affairs associated with survival. They go to the market, they choose the dresses for the family, they attend school board meetings, with or without their men, and they are care givers for the elders. So, I was gradually becoming Mama Scurry (my grandmother).

I was attending a council meeting when I was suddenly called. "Edith, leave whatever you are doing. Come home right away," the voice said. "It is Larmont," the voice added. My three children were the love of my life. Larmont on the other hand, was more rambunctious than my other two. Charles would often soothe my anger against Larmont by saying, "Honey, the boy is just like you. He is going to follow his star no matter what we say."

Placed in that prophetic way, I assumed Larmont's star will one day take a turn for Jerusalem. There he would behold God's heralds proclaiming peace unto all men of good will. Larmont had been a pain on my heart. I did not like his drinking.

"Will you tell me if Larmont is in jail or something?" I asked, my heart palpitating like that of an infant. "I don't know mom," the voice said.

"Well, somebody must know something," I urged gently, but fearing the worse.

"They are waiting for you mom," and the voice went out. It had done its job. These people are trained not to scare people or to say things that do not fall within their purview. I was in the dark, and yet I knew that my destiny was now in the balance. Something terrible had happened.

When I arrived, the whole tribe was waiting in the emergency room. Nobody seemed to know what to do, including Charles. They were waiting for me to make the decision. Larmont, who had been driving in a state of inebriation, had been in a fight and beaten with a baseball bat. During the fight his nose was crushed, his legs were broken and his jaw was crushed. While I was walking around his bed, he spit shattered teeth out of his mouth.

"Somebody must sign the consent form," said the attending nurse. The entire tribe looked aside.

"What are we going to do Edith?" Charles asked.

I recalled what my grandmother had taught me about my ancestors in Africa, the great Ashanti women. Even though the men are the spokespersons, and indeed they are most garrulous in debate, the wisdom comes from their matriarchs, the Asentewaa.

"The doctors are waiting for our decision," Charles added. So, it was that I made the decision.

Larmont had lived a reckless life, and this was it. This was not the time to preach. He was heavily sedated. I knew the operation would take at least two to four hours. There was no point of the tribe sticking around for the whole evening. Doctor Lansford help put Larmont back together with the assistance of other doctors as they filed in into the surgery, one by one. On a Saturday night, they were being called in from wherever they were. I prayed, and my prayer was answered. None of our doctors had left town that evening.

February 14, 2000 (Valentine's Day), I had a dream. The Holy Spirit revealed to me that Larmont would be involved in an automobile accident. Larmont would be admitted through the emergency room during my shift.

February 10, through February 14, 2000, every time I prayed tears rolled down my face. On February 14, I was working the third shift on Fifth West. I received four or five calls from the emergency room to requesting me to report to the ER. I was told that Larmont had been in an automobile accident. On the sixth call, my supervising nurse, Margie Mayo informed me that Larmont may be paralyzed, and I needed to come to the emergency room right away.

It was only through the strength of God, I completed my rounds. Afterwards, I went to the emergency room to see about Larmont. I found him lying in bed cursing out everyone around him.

I said demandingly, "Larmont, shut your mouth! Stop cursing right now!" Larmont was respecting of me, therefore, he stopped cursing at once.

Larmont's surgeon, Dr. John Sticken took us aside for a conference. He stated that Larmont had a fifty-fifty chance of living in a vegetative state. With our faith in God, we thanked the doctor and said that Larmont will be okay in spite of the diagnosis.

Lamont was not the best patient. He blamed us for his accident. For two years I prayed for God's grace. Eventually, the message was drilled by the Holy Spirit that he must follow his star, and find his calling. After two years of rehabilitation, he learned to use a wheel chair. He regained his cheerfulness, and returned to college. His three-year-old son was the apple of his eye. He never missed an opportunity to be with him, and they bonded. *God works in mysterious ways.*

Today, Larmont lives in Charlottesville, VA. with his oldest son, Kejuan. We are very proud of him. Larmont is self supporting. He will drive the six hours to visit his parents whenever he chooses to. God is still in control and he is just a prayer away.

L-R: Sabrina and Larmont
Back row: L-R-: Edith,
Charles and Jerome.
Photo taken in Hartsville, SC

L-R: Cameron and Kejuan
Larmont's boys.

Larmont and his dad

Larmont encourages son, Cameron
to get back in there... play football.

L-R: Larmont, Cameron and PJ.
Back row: Uncle James.
Easter dinner at Seaboard Rec.

Front row L-R: Cason and Lee.
Back row L-R: Fulton, Childs,
Smith, Reverend Mattison,
Morris and Butler. Pictured after
loading truck for New Orleans.

First Christmas dinner at
Magnolia Park, 2001. Over
two hundred people served.
Thanks to Leroy Crawford
and the late William McLean.

Pictured are the many volunteers
after Gage Street Park renovation.
County Councilwoman Childs returns
neighborhood to complete park.

CHAPTER-FOURTEEN
A Committed Life of Service
by Larry Wise

As a retired nurse, Edith has reached out to people to assist with their community issues. She has been very instrumental in getting water for the Troy community, establishing programs and events that are now being held annually. Edith receives calls from residents that are in need of assistance varying from utility bills, rent payments, legal issues, foreclosure and simple advice about other issues. Because of her known compassion and commitment to help others, Edith is called on constantly.

Mrs. Childs, through her vision, initiated annual Easter, Thanksgiving and Christmas Dinners, which is made possible by volunteers. All food items are furnished through donations. Each year these meals are made available to hundreds of residents in Greenwood County extending the spirit of sharing and giving.

Mrs. Childs began the county wide food drive collecting different items of food between December and January. Employees collect these food items from their places of employment, civic organizations and churches in conjunction with their food drive as a project for their particular organization. Greenwood City competes with Greenwood County to see who collects the most food. These nonperishable food items are donated to various agencies, such as the United Ministries, the Soup Kitchen and the Food Bank. Through these food drives the agencies are able to offer assistance to individuals and families, who are experiencing crisis, loss of jobs or long term illnesses.

Edith Childs has partnered with other politicians in making contributions to needy families in other areas as well. Mrs. Childs works as one of the coordinators of the Emma Gaskin Family Fun Day held at Magnolia Park in Greenwood. This fun day is filled with activities for children. They also receive educational information from The Red Cross and The Greenwood Fire Department. Entertainment is sponsored by local choirs and steppers. This is a day that families can come out and just enjoy themselves in memory of the late Emma Gaskin.

Have you ever wondered about the real effect members of Congress, House of Representatives, the Supreme Court, the president and other elected officials have on your life? Well I have, and oftentimes, I have come to the conclusion that not every elected official has the citizens best interest at heart of whom they are supposed to be representing. There is one official elected that is an exception. Our local county council member Edith S. Childs is one that fits the bill.

Edith Childs is a selfless individual exhibiting drive and a desire to always serve others. She has always been a model citizen that has an inner calling to assist others in whatever capacity she can. Her compassion to serve others was truly evident in her earlier years and she has continued with her involvement in the surrounding communities of Greenwood County. Edith is always initiating and maintaining involvement in community events and programs. She is very defiant in her stance to render service and support.

Mrs. Childs is a very unusual and unique individual. She is always eager to help others. She is concerned with local community issues, and she also has a concern with the political fabric of the nation. Edith encourages others to get involved with the political process locally, state wide and nationally.

Mrs. Childs, a county Councilwoman in District One, not only represents her people, but also represents others in other districts in political issues. Childs helped to coordinate the Back to School Bash. The Back to School Bash is held for hundreds of area children, which provides them with school supplies. Children are issued these supplies while playing games and having snacks. This school bash helps so many families that are unable to purchase supplies for their children. Groups from churches and neighborhoods arrive for the annual back to school bash.

Childs works diligently in organizing the county wide cleanup, which takes place throughout the county. Having a neighborhood that is clean and free of litter is an impediment to drugs and criminal activity.

Mrs. Childs works tirelessly leading the Crime Stopper campaign, trying to rid areas of crime, not only in her district but throughout Greenwood County. Crime Stopper signs were posted in areas of Troy, Callison, Bradley and Promised Land. A phone number is listed on the signs to use to report illegal activity privately. Residents that want to report criminal or suspicious activity may do so without providing their names.

After many phone calls regarding complaints from residents, Mrs. Childs worked diligently to have speed limit signs and caution lights erected in the community of Promised Land. After many accidents and two fatalities, this section of Highway 10 proved to be quite dangerous due to speeders. Finally, after years of pertinacity, the South Carolina Department of Transportation (SCDOT) responded to her.

Again, within the Promised Land Community, there was a section of the community that encountered a railroad that for many years blocked residents to and from their homes. There was only one road that led to this section of Promised Land Community and residents had no choice but to travel across the railroad. In the event of an emergency with the train blocking the roadway-it was just a matter of time before some type of catastrophe would occur. After years of complaints from residents, and Mrs. Childs, Greenwood County Council took action and passed a resolution which resulted in an alternative road being constructed. In 2007, thanks to the Goodman Family, the grand opening was held presenting the new road.

Again Mrs. Childs, acted as an advocate for the residents of Troy. After more than a decade, the town received a new fire truck to be used by volunteer firemen. Edith was extremely instrumental in this community receiving the new fire truck.

On an ongoing basics, Edith continuously works with others to make improvements within communities. She directs her energy in many directions including talks about new nursing home, designed specifically for the mentally challenged. Edith also directs her energy toward repairs of closed inner city swimming pools, the awareness of child abuse and neglect, the participation and promotion in the census. Childs is everywhere trying to do good.

In 2006, Mrs. Childs traveled to New Orleans. After hurricane Katrina crippled that city, she went there to show her compassion for others.

June 15, 2007, then Senator Obama visited the illustrious state and Greenwood, South Carolina. Amidst the few that gathered to meet him was County Councilwoman, Edith Childs. During that visit Mrs. Childs began to chant the words *Fired Up, Ready to Go*. The *Fired Up* chant became the hallmark throughout President Obama's campaign, *Fired Up, Ready to Go*.

The chant became known in Greenwood, and it was accepted throughout the United States. President Obama made a second trip to Greenwood, and he appeared at the Lander University sports arena. He asked if Edith would join him on stage. She began to lead the chant; *Fired Up, Ready to Go*. During the presidential election of 2008, Edith worked insurmountable hours. She often brought food to local volunteers working in the Obama campaign headquarters in Greenwood. She encouraged voters to register if they were not. Edith Childs County Councilwoman is an epitome of what mankind should emulate. The services she has rendered to Greenwood communities is beyond reproach. Unwavering, Mrs. Childs' commitment has touched the lives of many. Greenwood's citizens know that whatever services or assistance needed, they received them through the efforts of Mrs. Childs.

Edith is a pillar of the community and Greenwood County as she works with various agencies and individuals throughout the area. In February 2010, she was listed as one of the most influential black persons in the city and county of Greenwood.

Mrs. Childs has hosted many town hall meetings over the years to give residents of the community the opportunity to ask questions, discuss issues, voice concerns, complaints and or suggestions. These meetings have always proven to be beneficial to everyone by providing knowledge and understanding different issues.

Edith tries to do whatever she can to improve the quality of life for citizens throughout the community. Mrs. Childs is an active member of Morris Chapel Baptist Church in Greenwood, SC. She also takes time to visit other churches and participates in programs throughout the area. From participating as a speaker to going to dedication services to prayer breakfasts to missionary banquets to name a few, Edith is there.

Our Godly duties consist of serving others. We know from all of Edith's continuing work that she fulfills and exercises her spiritual duty.

MRS. EDITH S. CHILDS
A TRUE PUBLIC SERVANT

AS I THINK, I HONOR

I think of a public servant
doing good deeds and more
a born server, all the way to the core

I think of a public servant
with her humbleness and fight
one to never lose sight
that their strength to face opposition
is inherent to deal in every situation

I think of a public servant
with their loyalty and persistence
as they answer and to offer assistance

As I think, I honor the honorable
magnify the goodness
as they extend their services
and goodwill across the miles
creating opportunities
throughout communities... as I think
I THINK OF EDITH CHILDS.

Written by
Sandra Hall

L-R: Rep. Parks, Councilwoman Childs, Mayor James Peeler of Troy, SC and Carolyn Perrin during Edith's first Town Hall meeting in Troy.

Thanks to the Goodman family for donating the property for this project. Celebrating the dedication of a new access road, Ron McNair to Whitehall Road.

Childs mingling with guests prior to celebrating access road success.

Greenwood/Ninety Six NAACP celebrating 19 fully paid life members, under Chairwoman Edith Childs.

NAACP member's banquet dinner. L-R: B. Foster, O. Wright. Back L-R: Reverend Norman, D. Wright, E. Wright and R. Watson.

Pictured are L-R: Crime Stoppers members John Wilde and Donald Wright during Christmas parade.

The free Christmas dinner at R. L. Stevens Center.

Greenwood group waiting to have dinner at Marriott Inn in Williamsburg PA.

David and Alice Gaskin, Linda Chamberlain and Ann Gunby pose for picture at the Healthy Neighborhood Banquet.

Reverend and Mrs. Melvin Zeno of New Orleans, visits Greenwood after Katrina diaster.

Cathy Tolbert shares supplies during Back to School Bash held at Morris Chapel.

Reverend Mike Butler watches Glenn Rucker as he batters chicken.

CHAPTER-FIFTEEN
The Family's Story

Forty-two-years ago, I met this young lady wearing a mini skirt. A very good friend of mine, William *Crane* Robinson introduced me to her (Edith). We began hanging out on weekends. The more we hung out, the more I found myself liking her.

We double dated a few times with Crane and his girlfriend. I didn't know it at first, but I quickly found that Edith could actually out drink me. On weekends, we would buy rounds of drinks for the four of us. Edith drank everything before we could make it back to the table. Needless to say, every Saturday or Sunday, I would have to clean my car.

Edith really loved dancing. I couldn't dance at all. So she danced the night away as I stood holding up the wall, but I watched every step she made. After holding the wall up for so long, I decided that I would at least try a few steps. After being a wall flower, I got the hang of it.

After I became comfortable with our relationship, I needed to get myself a career. Earlier, I had made the decision to go into the Army to help defend my country.

I needed to get used to being in the military. Learning to dance was hard, and I thought that signing my name on the dotted line for the Army was going to be the hardest thing to do. I did not have any idea as to where my military assignments would take me, but this was still the farthest thing from my mind. My mind was set on whether my girl (Edith) would be here for me when I returned.

Needless to say, I returned home from military duty. We rekindled our relationship with much love and excitement. Two years later, September 4, 1971, Edith and I were married. We move into a rented house on Walker Street for our first two years of marriage. Later, we purchased a home in New Market Park where we continue to reside presently.

I didn't have any idea that my wife would become involved in politics and community services. This one little lady wears so many hats 'til I can't keep up with them or her. Nonetheless, I vowed to love her for richer or for poorer and for the rest of my life. Edith is truly the love of my life.

As age has taken over, our oldest granddaughter has now graduated from college. She has taken a very big step into adult life. As grandparents, we were excited and very proud of her accomplishment. I am truly grateful for Edith and all that she does for us and the community.

My Friend, My Wife–My Blessing
Charles Childs

I must say first that I thank the Lord for creating this wonderful woman in His image and calling her His own. Lord, I am delighted and grateful that you chose her to be our mother. I thank God for passing Abraham's blessing through my family and us the children of Charles and Edith Childs are proud to be recipients of God's continued blessings.

This is the woman who was my role model when I was a child. I looked up to her as if she was all that and then some more. I remember Mama stumping around the house in high heels and parading around in her clothes. I sometimes sang along with her and Betty Wright to the song *Clean Up Woman*. At times I danced with her as she stopped preparing our dinner to cut-a-step in the living room. There were other times when my dad would be jealous of all the fun we were having so he was forced to join in. Most of the time, he simply sat back and shook his head in agreement as his two girls put on a show for him. I knew that I had special parents. I had what some of our friends did not have two parents in the home.

It has been a blessing to call this lady, mother. I remember growing up as a child and experiencing the care my mother gave me. Selflessly, she gave to those who were in need. Our family was raised with traditional Christian values. We learned at an early age to put God first in everything. These instilled values have helped mold us into whom we are today. There were many nights my mother worked third shift but always found time to have our weekly Bible study. I will never forget our summer vacations away from Greenwood, which continually enhanced the true meaning of family.

It is truly a blessing to me to call (Edith S. Childs) Mama. She has not only been there for me and my siblings but for our father also. How she worked a full time job, raises three children and maintains a home for us I will never understand. But she did it and I see no regrets in her eyes. She is a blessing.

Mama is a woman that does not mind taking chances. Her motto is: *The Only Way Not to Succeed Is to Not Try*. My mother loved and nurtured us. I looked at my mother and I see a strong, determined, a faithful and devoted mother, daughter and wife. I described her as strong because she fought against all odds. She possessed such inner joy. She worked hard and sometimes played hard.

Mama was pregnant when she was still in high school. She was already counted out by society. She was determined to raise me the best she could alone and without my biological father having an active role in our lives. She realized her struggle and what it would take to rise above it all and to care for me. Although Mama sought financial assistance from my father, she did not receive any. She had a goal in mind and that was to prove to her family, the public but mainly herself that she would be there for me at all costs. There were other options that she could have taken. Mama chose to give birth to me and not abort me, her child and her dream.

Not only was she determined to raise me, she also was determined to better herself so as to have a chance in life. However, four years later, Mama was pregnant with my brother, Jerome. I remember living in a place where chaos reigned. Only a strong woman can start out with so many oppositions but conquer them all, one by one.

Faithful because it requires dedication, Mama made the decision to move from Philadelphia back to Greenwood, South Carolina with the assistance of my father, Charles Childs. Moving back to Greenwood prevented Mom from getting caught up in the fast lane of city life. My father, Charles loves my mom. After relocating back to Greenwood, we lived with my grandparents. They loved and adored me because I was their first and only grandchild.

My mother has always been one that worked and instilled in us the importance of working and being self-sufficient. She has always told me as her only daughter that it is important to have something to bring to the table. I should not wait on someone to take care of me but to be able to provide for myself and family. She would say, "Get established and whoever comes in your life will be an addition to what you already have." At that age, of course, I didn't understand. As an adult, I understand now. I have instilled the same values into my girls.

My mother always wore many hats before she actually started wearing hats. She worked hard (one hat), but I also remember the mother that took an interest in our education and social lives. No matter what, after school activities were part of our lives. They were always there! I remember so vividly when I was running track at Greenwood High School; only my mother would come bearing goodies: chocolates, peanuts, sodas, wafers and water. She said that the sugar would give us much energy for the race. As of this day, I am still riding high on that same sugar high. Letting the truth be known, most of the races I won but the few that slipped away, I guess I did not have enough sweets on those days. From the bleachers all I could hear was my personal cheerleader, my mom yelling, "Go! Jeannie, you can do it! She's catching up with you, Jeannie. Run! Run! Run Jeannie!" None of the other parents was as excited about the track meets as my mom was. This did not stop with me; it continued with my brothers, Jerome and Larmont. They played football and ran track.

As lovable as Mom is, she was very strict when it came to education. She believed that in order for us to be successful, an education was important. This was instilled voluntarily and sometimes involuntarily. I remember studying for a special spelling test. Mama was quizzing me on the words for that test. I kept getting the same word wrong, and my mother kept giving me the same answer. Jeannie, spell *Phi-la-del-phi-a!* I would say, it is *Phi-la-de-phi-a.*

"Jeannie, take this paper and go study your words and do not come back until you are ready," would be her reply.

Five minutes later I returned. "I got it, Ma," I said.

"Okay," she said. "Let's go."

Mama called out every word but Philadelphia. Last, but not least, came the word. Again, I said Phi-la-de-phia. "Jeanie, I thought you said you studied these words," out came the harshness in her voice.

"Ma, I did!" I said again.

"Now go to the room, study these words and don't you come out until I call for you!" Ma shouted.

This was the longest spelling quiz ever. She decided to teach me a lesson since I was in such a hurry to complete the quiz incorrectly. I have never forgotten how to spell Philadelphia again. Ma called me about two hours later. We could not watch television until our homework was done, checked and corrected... so much for that.

In my adult life, I practice what I learned as a child from my parents. Of course, I attribute it all to my parents. However, my mother believed that her little girl, her daughter should be exempted from the trials and tribulations of the world because she had already been through it for me. Sometimes we butted heads because I wanted to learn and see things for myself. I thought surely she can't understand because times have changed. Little did I know that she knew what she was talking about.

My mother is the initiator. She was responsible for some of the Civil Rights Movements in Greenwood prior, to Martin Luther King's Holiday being passed into law. I think back to my walking with Ma and the NAACP and what happened afterwards. Some people felt that we had arrived because of the Civil Rights Movement. I recall so vividly, the night after the march. We were returning home that night and feeling good and excited because we had done something that would pay off some day. That night I slept well. While I was still laying in the bed, the next morning, and just before breakfast, my father, as usual, went outside to get the newspaper. To his surprise and the entire family, our house had been sprayed with eggs. It was a horrible sight to witness.

Utilizing the quote that says, "This too shall pass," the family stood fast as to do nothing to promote any violence. After the egg incidence, we did not experience any other attacks until we were awakened to crashing sounds of glass.

Two white guys decided they would throw a beer bottle at our house. They broke several windows on the front of the house. One of the beer bottles broke the living room and landed in the middle of the floor. Another one fell in our front bedroom. I saw the car speeding away. Immediately, my parents jumped up and came running to see if everyone was all right. We did not know why this had happened to us. The police were called for both situations. Each time they filled out incident reports and took pictures.

We had never known what it felt like to be the target of racism before these two situations. Our parents never owned a gun but they did discuss purchasing one for protection. I don't recall them ever going out and actually buying one. Nonetheless, Mom and Dad seated Jerome and I down and explained that if anything happened to them, these were the precautionary measures to take. "What child wants to hear that something could possibly happen to their parents?"

I have many fond memories of my parents. My mother was the disciplinarian and the authoritative one. We knew when to find our dad; just when mom was exercising her right to be a parent, especially when she needed to correct or discipline one of us. As an adult, you can look back and say I am thankful for all of the corrections, because it molded me into the person that I am now.

My mother definitely knew her Bible. The Bible says, *spares the Rod but Spoil the child* then there was one that said, *Spare the Rod for Surely it will not kill them*. As a child, we wanted to really rewrite those verses. They did spoil us and she did not kill us. Thank you Jesus!

My grandmother and great-grandmother taught Mom so many things. She instilled them in us while we were at early ages. The one thing that Mom hated with a passion was a liar. That same thing still hold truth today. She always said, "If you are willing to lie, you will cheat; if you will cheat, you will steal." These were characteristics that Childs' children will not be guilty of doing. We heard the same lectures every day; Charles and I are instilling the same values in you.

Never in my life have I ever met another person as selfless as Mom. In her world, self comes last while others come first. The Bible says, *to not think of yourself higher than others or than you ought to*. I have seen Mom give others what she would not give to herself. She's one of those special people that just captures ones heart. She's a natural born mover and shaker—she won't stop until she gets the job done.

This quality speaks volumes to the woman that God created her to be.

I have seen many of the difficulties Mom faced in life, and I have also seen she looked up to God for an uplift. But most of all, God has enabled us through her, to seek God in our times of distress. If God said it then so will it be. *Before I formed thee in the belly I knew thee; and before thou camest forth out of the womb I sanctified thee, and I ordained thee a prophet unto the nations* (Jer 1:5 KJV).

God knew who she would be, what she would do and how she would do it. Mom in turn has pointed all the praise back to our Lord and Savior.

In times of extreme distress, Mom read to us this passage. *And we know that all things work together for good to them that love God, to them who are the called according to his purpose. For whom he did foreknow, he also did predestinate to be conformed to the image of his Son, that he might be the firstborn among many brethren. Moreover whom he did predestinate, them he also called: and whom he called, them he also justified: and whom he justified, them he also glorified. What shall we then say to these things? If God be for us, who can be against us?* (Romans 8:28-31 (KJV).

Our parents have loved us unconditionally even when we were growing up and coming into our own. They stood in front, behind and beside us as we found our way. My mother did not want us to make the same mistakes that she had made, especially me her one and only daughter. Needless to say, the entire time she was striving to keep me from a bad fate, I still fell into it! But Mom stood with my mistake always reminding me of *All scripture is given by inspiration of God, and is profitable for doctrine, for reproof, for correction, for instruction in righteousness: 17 That the man of God may be perfect, throughly furnished unto all good works* (2 Tim 3:16-17 (KJV). It corrects us when we are wrong and teaches us to do what is right.

This has taught me how to be a better woman, mother, sister, daughter, granddaughter, auntie, cousin, coworker and a friend. I guess you would say I'm an all around good person. I learned that love is what love does and now I am living that love is what love does.

My parents have passed these same values onto their grandchildren. They are just as supportive of them as they were of us. I love to see the gleam in my children's eyes: Lindaya, Lakeyia and Lorenzo II when they talk about their grandparents. Their grandchildren are very competitive and hate to lose at anything just like their Granny. They have seen the hard work from their parents and grandparents pay off in more ways than one. They realized if they think it, they can visualize it and it can be obtained.

As an adult, my mom still looks at me as her baby girl.

And I guess that she always will. The love of a mother never grows dull. She's my mentor, inspiration, love, mother, the sister I never had and my best friend. When I am down, she encourages me back up to functionality. She's the person that I consider to know everything about every thing. Mom is my confidant!

In 1988, I gave birth to my eldest child (their eldest grandchild), she was so supportive. She consoled me, rubbed my back and made me laugh. She told me what to expect and then sweetly relieved the nurses that were doing their job... because a mama nurse showed up. She took care of me as if she was on duty, except, she threw in some good ole tender loving care, (TLC). I love you, mom for all of the wonderful memories you have given me.

My parents adopted my husband into the family. From day one, they never referred to him as a son-in-law but as their son. Ma would call and talk to my husband and not to me sometimes. I wanted to know, why would my mother call and not talk with me. That's my Mama. He gets a kick out my jealousy. On the other hand, however, he has felt very secure whenever we are visiting with my family. Even when he runs into the ones that are not as settled as we are. They made him feel special and a part of our big fun-tas-tic and blessed family. We have an array of characters in our family and it shows when we get together. The laughter that comes forth will make you hurt yourself because we truly laugh at each other.

Train a child in the way he should go; and when he is old, he will not depart from it (Proverbs 22:6 KJV).

Thank you mom for living this proverb. Regardless, of how good or not so good I was, there was a standard that was established and we had to follow it. We have not departed from the biblical teachings because God was first and foremost in our lives. My mom has always said that she desires for all of us to be saved and live a life that is pleasing unto God. *And they said, believe on the Lord Jesus Christ and thou shall be saved and so shall thy house* (Acts 16:31 KJV).

My mother is a woman of prayer that does not mind bombarding heaven on behalf of her loved ones. I am so proud to call, Mr. Charles & Mrs. Edith Childs my parents.

Linda (Jeannie)

My parents always preached that if you make your bed hard, you have to sleep in it. The statement still rings as loud now as it did then. In our home dad was the quiet one and mom as you probably guessed was the out spoken one. I wanted my dad to punish me if I had done something I was not supposed to do. My mother did more talking, so I would feel bad and get punished at the same time. Mom worked as a Nurse and dad was a mill worker. There was always a parent at home, because dad worked the first shift and mom worked the third shift. This system worked until they retired.

Mom worked as a nurse during the day, and after getting her rest, she found time to start a program called Crime Stoppers (with the help of dad). As the years passed, she finally decided that she would run for Greenwood County Council. Mom has always had a drive for helping others. I remember mom helping the town of Troy get a new fire truck. I do not recall the price tag that was placed on the fire truck but she was instrumental in getting it done. Of course, we know that fire trucks do not come a dime a dozen. So it was a monumental task mom had gotten the fire truck for the town of Troy.

Our parents are an example for a successful marriage. While we were growing up, we always saw the two of them together. Constantly being together, demonstrated to us, their commitment of hanging in there for the long haul.

Mom used the system to work as a nurse for more than thirty years. She is a proven leader by showing her ability to listen. And Mom really listens well and intently to the many voices that sound off the needs of their communities.

Mom loves her family and this is noticed by helping my dad with his great Aunt Willie. They would stay the night with her, cooked and bathed her and do whatever was necessary on a daily basis until before she passed away. I knew they were tired because I could hear the tiredness in their voices when I would call to check on things. Mom and dad look at it as this is the plate that God has placed before us and this is what we now must do. Someday, perhaps, I too will have their kind of strength to do nonstop the things that mom and dad have done throughout the years.

I am married to Sabrina, and we have son, Jordan. I understand the importance of loving God first and then my family, as my parents taught us. Mom, I love you and dad I wish you the best with your new found passion to write.

Jerome and Family

As the last child in the family, my parents have been an inspiration to me and for me. As with all children, Maze (the musical group) said it best, it was *Joy and Pain.* My older sister and brother were there with us and then they left for college. It went from a house full of us to just me and our parents. Wow! What a change. Now my parents had all of the time to devote to me. I loved it when we had to share. I can say that I contributed to a lot of the joys and pains. Now, that I am grown and have children of my own, I can look back and say I understand why? My mother was very involved.

I remember attending high school and thinking that I was actually grown. My mother was very involved in my academics to the point that she escorted me to class ensuring that I was present, accounted for and paying attention. She believed the mind was a terrible thing to waste. And at that particular time I was wasting mine. I was embarrassed that she was sitting behind me in class, but Mom displayed no shame in her game. I learned to be a player; I had to learn the game. My mother beat me hands down, on all plays. However, this is one of the qualities that she displayed in showing her love for me. She would go to the ends of the earth for me to succeed.

My mother has been my nurse, mom and teacher on many different levels of my life. She assisted in rescuing me from myself. My parents encouraged and inspired me. However, there were boundaries that were displayed. I was the child and she was the adult! No questions! No speculations! No assuming! It was what it was! I recall while I was growing taller than my mom, I told her, "I am bigger than you are." Mom looked up at me, and she quickly pulled a chair from the kitchen table, stood on it and said, "I will stand on a chair and knock you out, Boy! Don't ever think that you will try me!" Needless to say, I never tried that with her again.

My parents have been through a lot with me. I thank God for them and their forgiveness. God's forgiveness is real. I thank mom for seeing the potential in me, which at that time I did not see it in myself.

As a parent now, myself, there is so much that we must endure. I was in college and had two sons that were born six months apart. Instead of her encouraging me to stop college and get a job. Mom encouraged me to bring my son to her so that his mother and I could continue our higher education. How s-e-l-f-l-e-s-s was that? Most parents would say you laid down and got them now take care of them.

"You are my baby and you are grown!" How much more precious and special could she become? What people do not realize is that this is who she is all of the time! Many times, I felt that she gave so much of herself to others and they were unappreciative. I encouraged her at times to stop doing it. She would look at me and say, "I do what I do because I love doing it. This is what God has blessed me to be." Although, I am a man of many words, she left me speechless.

My parents attended every sports event I participated in. I could hear her squeaking voice cheering me onto victory. She was my personal cheerleader. She would always conclude by saying, "That's my baby!" It amazed me to see the lengths that my parents would go for me. They climbed the highest mountain just to see me succeed in life.

On that dreaded day I was involved in a car accident was when I saw her strength shine more than before. I lay helpless, glad to see my parents come through that emergency room door. My mother ran to my side to aid me through my suffering. I saw the look of anguish and anxiety on her face, yet she poured out her love just as a mother would. I knew that my diagnosis must have been worse than I had anticipated. Mom consoled and comforted me through every stage of recovery I went through. Only God could allow her to contain herself as the doctors gave their prognosis that I was paralyzed from the waist down. Mom nevertheless, researched until she found a hospital that could deal with my anger issues about my paralysis. They strengthen, encouraged and inspired me to be the best I can be despite being in a wheelchair. My mother is a God send.

How my parents put up with me through all of hysteria, I don't know. I was now able to see the errors of my ways. I must have been unsufferable. I was a know it all and this was what got me into the wheelchair. But thank God for a loving mother and father.

I never understood how she could be sick and never take her body into consideration. When it would come to others and their welfare she simply said, "I don't have time to be sick. There's too much work to be done and not enough time to do it. Larmont, you are more than welcome to join me. I won't have as much to do then."

Mom has always been a strong woman of faith. I know that it was her answered prayer as to why I am still here. She could easily win the *Good Samaritan Award*. Mom doesn't care whom she helps. If there is a need, she is there through every good or bad that comes her way. The bad things are what taught her to press on and pray. Her ability to endure heartaches, pains, shame and blame enabled her to beat the odds.

My dear mother was a consistent help in my time of need, and as I stated earlier, she assisted me with both of my boys. I could never thank her enough for all that she has done for us. The greatest gift that I can give back to her is to be there for my boys just as she was for her kids. My parents have been a standing foundation for me when I couldn't stand on my own. Only God knew what He was doing when He created them.

She is who she is because she loves what she does.

Larmont Childs

Grandchildren and nephew, D. Sanders.

Linda (Jeannie), accepting academic trophy.

Sanders, Wright and Childs family gathering.

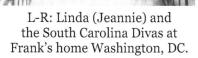

L-R: Linda (Jeannie) and the South Carolina Divas at Frank's home Washington, DC.

Charles takes a break while touring Washington, DC.

Charles and Edith during Charles' class reunion prom that never was.

Lorenzo and Linda Brown family.

Edith Childs 2011 Woman of Wisdom .

Kejuan posing after church.

Childs family cruising the waves.

Pictured is Larmont, Tiffany and Cameron.

CHAPTER-SIXTEEN
When Politics Began

In the mid 1980's, I began thinking about a possible political career. I started out by observing how the politics in Greenwood worked. Many politicians that ran were rumored to be a part of the *Good Ole Boy System.* These good old boys had the power to open the doors for those that were deemed acceptable and shut the doors on those that were deemed unacceptable. Perhaps, someone made a statement to me that I should know that politics is a game for the *good ole boys.* I felt that there comes a time when one must take a stand for what they believe in. Why not little old me... Edith S. Childs, a woman.

The first position I held was at Matthews Elementary School as Vice President of the Parent Teacher Organization (PTO). For the next two of years, I was elected, by the parents for two School Improvement Councils [sic]: Brewer Middle School and Southside Junior High School. I was told that I could only serve at one school. I wanted to be of assistance to both schools. I found the decision hard to make. However, I finally made the decision to serve at Brewer.

I felt the need to serve because I wanted to make a change in students' lives. Charles and I were always hands on parents. We took time to visit our children's school and their teachers on a regular basis. Neither administrators nor teachers were ever forced to call us concerning disciplinary action for our children. We were always present and on the grounds. If we could make a positive impact for our children, surely we could do the same for other children. While serving on [sic] school board, I became involved in school activities such as fund-raisers. There were times when I witness injustices to both black and white students.

In 1993, three seats opened on the school board. Twelve people were running for the same seats. I ran and I came in fourth place. Although I lost, this was the beginning of my political career.

The first lesson I learned was campaigning was hard, but it is very important. It meant that I must go out and meet the people, talk about real issues and share my ideas. But the most important, I had to listen to my constituents. Because I listened, I quickly became a p*eople person.*

In 1994, I decided that I would file again for the School Board, but this time I made sure that all of my T's were crossed and the I's dotted. Who enjoys losing? Not me! Needless to say I won! I served on the school board for four years. I was there until I decided to run for Greenwood County Council District One. I prayed constantly and endlessly about running for this office. Of course, I discussed my candidacy with my husband. My mind was fixed on being in politics. My mind set was "I am in this to win!" I prayed to God for direction as to what to do. He answered my prayer-it was okay for me to run and run I did.

Four candidates ran against me in the primaries. After an exhausting and tiring campaign, it proved that hard work pays off. During the general election with opposition, I won the County Council seat for District One.

I continue today representing District One on the County Council. I am very grateful to my constituents for their continued support. There is so much to learn, and so many issues that need to be rectified. To address change, one must affect research, investigate, inquire and always seek the people's knowledge. I attended various workshops in Columbia, Myrtle Beach and Hilton Head Island, all of which is located in South Carolina. I did not care about the distance because I knew that knowledge was power. The workshops enabled me to know firsthand the changes that were going to take place. I was able to distribute the information to my communities sooner rather than later.

Everyday was not always a gratifying one. I struggled with politics and the views of others that displays a harsher side. It would have been grand if everyone thoughts were alike. I can even understand if their thoughts were honorable, righteous, uplifting, boosting and respectful. Perhaps, this is wishful thinking. Just like eyes, everyone has them, so the same goes for opinions. As my grandmother prophesied to me, I am living out that prophesy today. I recall often what my grandmother said, "One of these days, gal, you are going to be with them big folk uptown." This has always stuck in the back of my mind, and it seems to always come up at the most inopportune time.

I have withstood many challenges coupled with much negativity. I must remain strong and prayerful to deal with pressure and the nay-sayers. I must never forget that racism still exists. All of these things one will be faced with just as the poor and hungry will be among us, so will racism and prejudices. God is still in charge. He is my source of strength and power through all things.

School Board members Ken Moody and Edith Childs discuss and
analyze the school budget.

SCHOOL BOARD AND SUPERINTENDENT 1998

(One of Edith's Campaign Flyers)

When you vote on November 5th, remember that a vote for Edith S. Childs is a vote for your child.

Greenwood School District #50 Board of Trustees District Four

If reelected I will work to achieve these goals:

1. To assure that each child attains an education that will enable him to become a successful and productive citizen.
2. To hold administrators and teachers accountable for educating all children to their potential.
3. To promote the hiring of minority teachers etc. (male and female).
4. To decease teacher-pupil ratios (where necessary).
5. To be consistent with punishment for all students.
6. To decrease dropout rate, expulsion and teen pregnancy.
7. To require expelled students to attend conflict-resolution workshops before readmission to a District 50 school.
8. To execute a superb line of communication between administrators, parents and students.
9. To provide a safe school environment that is free of violence and drugs for all students.
10. To give my utmost ability to serve the community, and do the right thing by all-school staff and parents, student and citizens of the community.

EXPERIENCED
CAPABLE
COMMITTED

CHAPTER-SEVENTEEN
The Journey Toward 2008

April 13, 2007, I had the honor of meeting Senator Barrack Obama at a Black Caucus Dinner in Columbia, South Carolina. We sat quietly waiting for the guest speaker to make his grand entrance. Finally, Senator Obama entered the room. *He is one fine-looking man.* He is a poised speaker that speaks in an elegant way. He is captivating to just listen to.

During his speech, he formally announced that he was a presidential candidate. He stated that he needed our support to bring change to America. As I listened, one statement immediately caught my attention. Senator Obama spoke passionately about Mrs. Annie Cooper. Mrs. Cooper is 105-years-old. Senator Obama met Mrs. cooper during one of his campaign rallies. Senator Obama spoke about how she had inspired him to keep running for the highest office in the United States... the Presidency.

On June 15, 2007, Senator Obama made a promise to Representative Anne Parks. He stated, "I will come to Greenwood, South Carolina." He is an honorable man because he kept his word.

My grandma Scurry used to always tell me, "Edith, all you have is your word. If you tell someone something, do your very best to keep your word. Once you break your word, people will consider you to be a liar. They will not believe anything else that you say." Senator Obama's word was his bond.

Presidential candidate Barack Obama's arrival plans were being plotted and processed prior to anything being put into writing. The guest list would only permit forty people to attend the banquet. My name was on the list. It was my will because of continued blessings from God, I chose to bless someone else with my pass.

Needless to say, I was bumped off the list due to my inability to see into the next moment. I simply stated, "It's okay. I will come with the Sheriff Department."

While I stood in one of the small Greenwood Civic Center rooms, listening to Obama's speech, I saw clearly that he had good vision for America. The Bible says that you should *wear your vision and make it plain.* Senator Obama explained his plan and made it plain. I was excited for what was to follow this man called Barack Obama. After his speech, he casually spoke with each guest.

As Senator Obama greeted the guests, Robert Tinsley said aloud, "Mrs. Childs, you should lead the chant *Fired Up Ready to Go* for the Senator."

My respond was, "No! Robert, I did not come here for that. I just want to welcome Senator Barack Obama to Greenwood."

"Edith, you really need to rejuvenate and revive him. It will encourage him for the road ahead. You need to sing *Fired Up Ready to Go*," Robert continued.

After Robert's nudging, he gave me the cue to sing *Fired Up*. I agree everyone needs encouragement from times to time and to know there is someone standing in agreement with them. Needless to say, I began singing *Fired Up Ready to Go*. Five of us started singing, Reverend Harrison, Jean Robinson, Betty Boles, Clara Sheppard and I.

Senator Obama was speechless. He could not help but be curious as to who were singing *Fired Up, Fired Up, Ready to Go, Ready to Go*. After pulling me out of the crowd, he proceeded to give me the biggest hug.

I was delighted that it brightened up his day during such a rugged campaign trail. I did not have a clue, however, this chant was ringing so deeply in him so much that he adopted it as one of his campaign slogans.

I received the first call from Mrs. Barbara Jackson, the wife of former president of Lander, Dr. Larry Jackson. She was in Iowa visiting her daughter-in-law to be. She had heard the story behind the chant on the news.

She could not wait to call me. I didn't think it was a big deal. I simply thought how nice it was that Senator Obama was using these words as his campaign slogan. I was actually pleased that it was something he considered useable. His campaign took off like a rocket after its adoption.

My plans were to attend the National Democratic Convention, which was held in Denver, Colorado. I purchased a ticket with my private credit card because I was determined to be there.

Edith S. Childs
Candidate For
National Democratic
Convention Delegate
May 3, 2008

Hello! Hello! I am Edith Childs from Greenwood, SC. I need your vote to become a delegate to the National Convention for Senator Barack Obama.

Hearing Sen. Obama speak during the Black Caucus Dinner in April was a humbling experience for all present. He has a sincere desire to help the jobless, homeless, to provide healthcare for all citizens, stabilize Social Security, provide quality education for our children, and most importantly unifying our country. Now you have been energized to be **Fired Up – Ready to Go – for Senator Obama to Win – "Yes He Can Win!**

How have I supported Senator Obama?
- Inspired the "Fired Up Ready to Go" slogan used by Sen. Obama's campaign during a brief stop in Greenwood, SC
- Extended southern hospitality and worked closely with the Sen. Obama's Greenwood Office staff and supporters during the SC Democratic Primary; transported voters to the poles
- Stuffed Thanksgiving bags for seniors and disenfranchised citizens with food and Obama literature during Greenwood's Day of Greens
- Canvassed communities campaigning for Sen. Obama

My Personal Experience
- Currently serving as Greenwood County Councilwoman for District 1 and previously served on Greenwood School District #50 Board
- Founder and organizer of Greenwood Crimestoppers
- Yearly supply hundreds of children with back to school supplies
- Annually co-sponsor dinners for the disenfranchised during Easter, Thanksgiving and Christmas
- Active member of Morris Chapel Baptist Church and Health Care Coordinator for the Little River Baptist Association

"Fired Up – Ready To Go"

I am in support of Edith Child being a National Democratic Delegate (NDD) to represent South Carolina at the NDC. Edith inspired Barack Obama with his *Fired Up and Ready to Go* campaign. She is known around Greenwood as the *Hat Lady*.

Representative Ann Parks
House of Representatives, SC

Please be advised I hereby highly recommend Mrs. Edith Childs as an Obama delegate to the NDC. She is a long time party loyalist with great commitment. I was present when she met the Senator. She was subsequently assumed a key role in the campaign. As Executive Committeeman for Greenwood County, I fully endorse Edith Childs' candidacy. She will bring great honor to our party at said convention.

Attorney Robert J. Tinsley

Across America, people are eager to meet The lady in the *Church Hat*, who has inspired us all with her traditional cheer, *Fired Up Ready to Go*. Edith has put SC democrats in the national eye. We must send Edith Childs. Her work in her community, her church and as a County Councilwoman represents the best American values. She is truly an inspiration and a great Democrat.

Larry A. Jackson
Barbara A. Jackson

I am pleased to recommend Mrs. Edith as a delegate to the National Democratic Convention. I have known Mrs. Childs for several years as my County Councilwoman, fellow church member and a personal friend. She is people-oriented, focused, a community organizer and a hard worker.

Edith is the driving force for the *Elect Obama Campaign* in Greenwood County. She worked tirelessly prior to the primary election and continues to keep his name alive. She is responsible for the *Fired Up Ready To Go* slogan that the Senator use from time to time during his campaign.

Anne J. Gunby

Life-long residents of Greenwood and pastor of Mt. Zion Baptist Church, we have witnessed her integrity, and distinctive qualities of mind and feelings Mrs. Childs has exhibited for the people of this county and state. Her amazing ability to organize an event or project and bring people together for a common cause has been demonstrated by her many accomplishments. She has tireless worked for Barack Obama's campaign and energized others to become vigorously active. One notable example is her famous *Fired Up Ready To Go* chant, which became the Obama campaign chant.

Reverend Bernard White
Mrs. Willie White

As the Pastor of Mt. Zion AME Church in Promised Land, for the past eleven years, and Chairman of the Board of the Promised Land Enrichment and Development Center, I have founed Councilwoman Edith Childs to be a great asset to the Greater Greenwood Community. She is diligent and tireless in her work as she serves she serves the constituents of District One. She has excellent character and impecable integrity. What she tells you she will do; she strives wholeheartedly to do that. I, Reverend James E. Speed, Sr. believe that she would serve us well as a delegate to the 2008National Democratic Convention.

Reverend James E. Speed, Sr.

Mrs. Childs' vivacious spirit and willingness to commit her limited time to project geared toward bettering our community are unending. She always has a smile and open heart for not only close friends and relations, but to people whom she has just met, her lively character and sparkling wit draw people to her on a regular basis. As an area leader, Mrs. Childs does not hesitate to involve herself with issues both her and her delegates deem appropriate and does so wholeheartedly. Well known for her enthusiastic chant *Fired Up Ready To Go*, which became a tagline for Senator Barack Obama's presidential campaign, Mrs. Childs continues to be a large force in a small frame both locally and nationally.

Julene W. Fisher

Edith waiting to hear Presidential candidate Barack Obama at the National Democratic Convention in Denver, Colorado.

Thank you Judge Betty J. Williams for your kindness in escorting me, during my interview with CBS. Edith poses with limousine driver at Columbia College in New York.

Charles and Edith on their way to the Presidential Inauguration of 2008.

Brian Pitts poses with Edith before CBS interview.

L-R: Pictured with Edith, Pat (Edith's beautician), Lynn (Edith Jewelry designer), and Suzy Holloway.

Migil (NY) reporter pictured with Edith at Morris Chapel Baptist Church-Greenwood, SC.

Edith pictured with workers at the Obama campaign headquarters in Greenwood, SC.

Placement of the Brewer High School Historical site Monument class members of 1966.

Brewer High School class of 1966 reunion.

L-R: Jerome, Charles and Sabrina. Jerome's day of graduation from St. Leo University, 2006.

Edith accepting the Presidential Medallion 2005 at Piedmont Technical College.

Edith smiles after receiving her Criminal Justice Degree in 1999.

Mr. & Mrs. Willie Randall   Mr. & Mrs. Charles Edith Childs

Pictured is Dr. Tompkins' Family:
L-R: wife, Mary Lee, daughter,
Connie and their Son, Duncan.

The mural is Dr. Tompkins.

Dr. & Mrs. Robert C. Moore

CHAPTER-EIGHTEEN
The Virginia Girls (Philomela)

Edith Childs' story of her encounter with President Obama on the campaign trail struck a chord with Philomela. Philomela is a female vocal ensemble in Washington DC. Through music Philomela sings of the journeys of women and of their joys and struggles as they search for peace, beauty, meaningful relationships and social justice in their life and others. Philomela was inspired to give voice to Mrs. Childs' story through music.

Our journey began following the excitement of President Obama's election, when Philomela director, Kathy Kessler Price, conceived of a concert that would include songs about hope, peace, inclusion and patriotism. Myra Binns Bridgforth, a poet and singer with Philomela, was asked to write a poem to be put to music for the group. When reading about the election on President Obama's website, she was moved by his story about his encounter with Mrs. Childs, and how he was inspired by her. Edith Childs inspired Myra, too, who chose this story for her poem.

Myra describes this transformation from a story about social justice and determination through one woman's story to a work of art.

In all of my poems, my intentions are to capture a moment in time, what it looks like, sounds like and feels like-to be in a particular moment. Writing a poem about change and hopefulness in our nation and the world was a brilliant and really impossible leap. Seeking inspiration, I started reading speeches that President Obama had made during his campaign that were published on his web site. This is where I discovered the Fired Up... Ready to Go Lady.

From the inspiration of her story, I wrote a prose poem that ends with the words that President Barack Obama used to end his story about Edith Childs. He said that he was changed in the moment when he heard her chant. In that moment he was glad to be in a small town in South Carolina on a rainy day when he was really tired. He said that "one voice can change a room, and if one voice can change a room, it can change a city, and if it can change a city, it can change a state, and if it can change a state, it can change a nation, and if it can change a nation, it can change the world."

Philomela commissioned composer, Ian Coleman to create the music for Myra's poem. He tells his story about transforming the poem into song.

I liked two things in particular about it–first, the fact that it was based on an actual event on the campaign trail, and secondly, that it quoted actual words from President Obama. Looking at the text, I felt that it fell into three sections. The first part is descriptive of the situation, in which the event took place, the second the chant itself, and the final section, the words of Obama in response to the chant. The chant I set in a recurring-layered pattern that I hoped might at least mimic the actual chant, and the words of Obama just fell into a natural rhythm that almost suggested their own melody.

Philomela eagerly embraced this song, and the story of the woman behind it. Our mission, part of which are *women's voices reflecting women's voices* had renewed energy and meaning. The song's title, "Change" was changing us. And then there was more change. In the midst of rehearsing this song the article *A Hundred Anxious Days*, featuring Edith Childs, appeared in The Washington Post. The President she helped to elect had served for a hundred days and the Greenwood, SC Councilwoman, whose chant *Fired Up Ready to Go* ignited a Presidential campaign, was now dealing with the depressing, frustrating aftershock in her own town from the economic collapse. The article went on to further describe how, just as Edith Childs had bucked up a candidate during a tough time in the campaign, so, too, was she using every resource in her power to respond to her neighbors and fellow citizens reeling with problems from unemployment.

Another chord was struck. Edith Childs was becoming a legend to Philomela! This remarkable woman, we needed to meet and invite her to be our guest of honor when we debut our song about her.

Maggie Rheinstein, another singer of Philomela describes her first phone conversationas:

The person who returned my call, to my immense delight, was humble and warm, but still showed the flint of her determination. When Mrs. Childs heard about our song project, "Change," she immediately embraced the idea of coming for the debut by declaring *The Lord has sanctioned it*. I will never forget how that contact made me feel an immediate connection with Edith, who was equally religious, forceful, idealistic and personable. She let me know how powerfully proud she was that we had decided to tell her story in performance. Edith was a very real person grounded in political reality, but unswerving in her belief that the *righteous will always prevail*.

The weekend of our concert, Philomela met Mrs. Childs and her cousin Miranda Boozer at Maggie's house. Maggie says:

Edith was dressed in an incandescent green outfit, with a casual hat for dinner at my house with many of the Philomela's singers. She's a masterful storyteller, and she had us riveted as she explained how the *Fired Up Ready to Go* chant evolved from the Civil Rights era. Activists would walk through voting areas calling out to African American citizens, who might be too scared to vote. The chants, repeated by the voters in a call and response pattern, cheered the citizens. Continuing the chants, they came out of the shadows to brave the polls. Edith's formidable story-telling skills carried all of us. There was immediacy to the experience! We were there with her and the voters. We also felt the direct connection between those early calls to vote and her chant that became President Obama's winning campaign slogan.

Edith has a quick sense of humor and a great sense of timing. She has amazing personal charm and story-telling prowess. The best story she told that evening was the one when Senator Obama reached her on her cell phone to ask her permission to put her chant on his website. On an errand at the Dollar Store, Edith answered the phone call from a number she did not recognize. The caller introduced himself as Senator Obama. Edith does not tolerate prank callers so she admonished the caller in no uncertain terms, to not *waste her time with such foolishness.*

While Obama chuckled, he also explained to Edith that he had gotten her information from her office in Greenwood. Edith immediately responded with a voice full of charm and humor, "Hello, Senator Obama." This story was quintessential Edith-feisty, fierce and full of fun.

We bonded that night, and felt as though we were entertaining an old friend, not someone we had just met and had admired from afar.

The evening with Edith was transforming for many of us. It echoed what Myra had already written to the members of her church in her invitation to the concert.

I want to stand up for taking responsibility for what I can do. I want to stand up with my church community, supporting charitable groups, holding each other up in our losses, our worries, our plans for right now and for the future. I want to keep writing poems that express what I feel about life and what it is like to live it. I want to sing songs and write songs about what is possible and to celebrate. Join me in practicing hopefulness and celebrating the moment.

As the audience filled in for our performance, the next day one person stood out. Dressed to the nines with a marvelous lime suit and magnificent matching hat, our guest of honor had outfitted herself regally. Philomela was *Fired Up and Ready to Go*! As we prepared to begin Edith's song, we were electrified by the energy she brought to the room. The highlight of our concert came as Edith, after hearing "Change," led an enraptured audience with her chant.

Kathy recalls:

I had already asked Edith before the concert if she would care to speak to the audience during the concert, and she had demurred, seeming a bit shy and reluctant to take center stage. The performance was so palpably exciting for us, and the spirit in the room so exhilarating that I believe she was prompted by that same spirit to step out. Edith won the hearts of everyone there, as she told her story of the "fired up" chant, and then led Philomela and the audience in a rousing rendition of it. I felt as if we were kindred souls, and that each woman in Philomela and in the audience and each man there as well, had bonded in a common cause of believing we could make a difference in this world. Words and music, music and words – those are powerful combinations.

Sitting in the audience was one of Philomela's former members, Mary Alyce Delaplane who describes her impressions from the concert:

I had nothing to do with the experience of Edith or her song until the afternoon of the concert. I was struck by the singleness of purpose and spirit in the church, as were all the Philomela singers. But what also impressed me were the differences. I remember Edith getting up, somewhat reluctantly at first, to speak to us in her matching lime green dress and huge hat that almost dwarfed her. This little lady, so small in stature and so towering in spirit! And within a minute, she absolutely commanded that huge sanctuary. She was teaching us, a predominately white audience, and her chant from her experience as a black woman fighting a Civil Rights battle, and she was so much more powerful in her delivery than we were in our responses. I simply marveled at the strength that this one, lone woman could summon and which we in the audience, even with our numbers, were not able to match. I felt timid and somewhat inadequate in her presence.

Edith's voice for change echoed throughout Philomela's extended family, as well. One by one, sons, daughters, mothers and cousins became inspired by Edith's message. Maggie's daughter was so enthused about the dinner guest coming to her house that she single-handedly prepared a wonderful feast. Myra's mother welcomed all of us at her house for a get together celebration following the concert. Accompanying Edith on all her excursions in DC was her cousin, Miranda Boozer, and for the concert, her nephew came as well. They brought their own stories to this wonderful journey we were taking together. Kathy's son joined us for Philomela's second outing with Edith. Philomela singer, Judy Kane, was helped by her daughter to document this journey.

Months went by and Edith kept in contact with Maggie from time to time. Last fall she called to say that she and her husband Charles were coming to DC again and this time they were going on a White House tour, and she wanted as many of us from Philomela to come with her on the tour as possible.

Maggie recalls:

We had hoped to sing *Change* for the President at some point, and we had received some encouraging communication from the office of the First Lady, who had considered attending the debut concert until she had a scheduling conflict. Our visit included our director, Kathy, lyricist Myra, composer Ian Coleman and a few singers, enough to cover all the parts in case we would finally have an opportunity to sing *Change* at the White House! We were not able to sing, but we all felt a deep, profound honor to be walking through the White House with the lady who was so instrumental in placing Obama there.

Ian, who had not come to the debut, reflects on this outing with Edith:

That will be a memorable day on many levels for me, an Englishman! But I think particularly in sitting down and hearing Edith tell (for the first time to me) the story of the rainy night where the chant had been used that I later set to music. It was both surreal and heartwarming in the same moment. I think it also reminded me that art has a role to play in helping to remember and immortalize these sorts of significant events. And I applaud Philomela for developing this idea and seeing it through and feel honored to have been asked to be a part of it on so many levels.

The echo of one voice reverberates in many ways to inspire, to transform, to change our lives and to change the world. The chant voiced by civil rights leaders encouraged African-Americans to vote. Edith Childs' voice as she repeated that chant more than forty years later, changed Obama and inspired his election campaign, which led to his victory and change for America. Edith Childs inspired Philomela, as well, to give voice to that spirit of hope, determination and change through song.

Change

Lyrics by Myra Binns Bridgforth
Music by Ian Coleman

A video recording of the first rendition of "Change" can be
heard by going to the Philomela website at
www.philomelavoices.org.

Walked into a room in a town
Small town in South Carolina
Filled with fine folks he didn't know
Just because he said he would.

And then the bright chant oh, my yes
Chant to his ear she sweet shouted.

Fired up – ready to go,
Fired up – ready to go,
Fired up – ready to go,
Fired up – ready to go.

Now, bless her soul
He is grateful to be here, right here

It shows what one voice can do
That one voice can change a room
And if one voice can change a room,
It can change a state, it can change a nation

For it shows what one voice can do
That one voice one voice can change a room
And if one voice can change a room,
It can change a state,
It can change a nation
It can change a world
It can change a
You can change the world!

Edith pictured with Philomela girls.

Morris Chapel Sunday school visits Birmingham Civil Rights Memorials.

L-R: Cameron, Pj and Dee rests during visit to Birmingham Civil Rights Memorials.

Edith pictured with first black registered nurse, Pauline Bray Fletcher of Alabama.

L-R: Dee, Cameron and Pj poses in front of Civil Rights attack dogs.

top: During visit to nation's capital Edith is captured standing in front of Sojourner Truth.

right: Edith stand beside Dr. Martin Luther King monument during visit at the nation's capital.

Some supporters that have made a difference in the community.

Daisy's Country Kitchen receiving their plaque for community service.

Tonya and Marie of Food Lion receives plaque for their community service.

Jeremy of Food Lion receives community service plaque.

The Golden Girls serving meals at R. L. Stevens Center.

Edith shown with Little River, Mt. Zion AME, Flint Hill, Bikers United, Fast Kats and other brothers posing after cooking a meal for the needy.

CHAPTER-NINETEEN
Our Date With the President

My cousin, Edith Childs has always been an integral part of me and my family's life. As long as I can remember, she has been my self-appointed big sister although she is my first cousin. I recall my mother explaining to Edith the importance of education. While Edith was obtaining her high school diploma, my mother stated that was just the start. All that she needed to do was simply apply herself, and she would get through it with ease.

That is exactly what Edith did. She graduated earning her high school diploma. Quickly and assuredly Edith moved onto bigger and better things that life had in store for her. Although, the family traveled with my father during his twenty-two-year military career, we seem to rest for periods in Greenwood, South Carolina. My father tours took him to Korea, France, Vietnam, Germany and throughout the continental United States.

Periodically, as family we reconnected. When I saw Edith, of course we would catch up with her affairs, whether she was geared to school, college, nursing, private investigations, voluntary work, the County

Council's work or just being a political activist. I am not sure how she found the time to do all these well-worth adventures and maintain a marriage, raise a family and a political career. I admire her for her accomplishments. Certainly there are yet many more to come.

During one particular weekend, I began to see Edith in a totally different light. A call came late that night about 11pm. (If you know Edith, she does most of her strategical planning late at night or during morning hours).

"Hello Cuz, I am coming to Vienna, Virginia for the weekend. Will you be in town?" Edith inquired.

"I live in Alexandria, Virginia. However, it is close to Vienna. I will check my schedule," I replied.

After checking my calendar, I advised Edith, "I do not have any plans that cannot be rearranged. In fact, I am at your disposal."

With my cousin, it's all or nothing. So I knew I was in for something. I picked her up from Old Towne Alexandria, Virginia-the Amtrak train station.

After brief greetings, hugs and kisses, I whisked Edith away. I was due to return to work at D.C. Pretrial Services Agency, which is located on 7th and Indiana Ave. NW Washington, D.C. From my tenth floor office window, I pointed out how close I was to the new administration's transition team building. We talked about how often I was interrupted by sirens. These sirens always announced the president's arrival or his departure from the train station in Alexandria, VA, which he took to Washington, D.C.

Edith informed me that she had been invited to dinner in Vienna by Maggie Rheinstein.

"Who is Maggie?" I asked.

Edith replied saying, "Maggie is a lady I met over the telephone in response to a story in the newspaper of me starting the *Fired Up Ready to Go* chant used during President Obama's campaign."

My question was, "What chant?"

We further discussed the itinerary for the evening. Our original plan was that Edith would make the introductions, and a little small talk then leave. Little did we know that Maggie and the other ladies of Philohela were awesome. We sat on the family couch (configured for conservation), and talked like old friends, who had not seen each other in years. As quickly as we were seated, the questioning started.

"What is he like?"

"How did you meet him?"

"What do you do?"

"Where is Greenwood, South Carolina?"

To my surprise these ladies were truly interested in my cousin... what was I missing? I listened intently as Edith told her story about a Democratic Senator Obama, who rolled into Greenwood, South Carolina one rainy Friday morning.

Senator Obama came in at the request of a South Carolina representative in hopes that he could gain support as he ran for office. Edith stated that a small group of city officials and other local dignitaries were gathered to meet Senator Obama to discuss issues that pertained to South Carolinians... particularly Greenwood. During the meeting, Edith stated there were light conversations, coupled with handshakes and pats on the back.

As the Senator's time was winding down, Edith was encouraged to start the old African American chant used in the late sixties as marchers prepared for the Civil Rights rallies. Edith began ever so faintly; "Fired Up." She waited for the proper response from the dignitaries; "Ready to Go." This was all that it took for Edith to repeat her part again and again until the roar grew louder with each round.

The Senator, who was scheduled to depart for other campaign stops started looking around to see who had started the chant. Completely moved by the chant, Senator Obama and his staff remained just a bit longer to share the enthusiasm of the people.

According to Edith, not long after the meeting with Senator Obama, she received a telephone call. The caller stated, "Hi, I am Senator Barack Obama." She stated aloud, "I don't have time to play games." She thought it was a hoax. However, she listened and it was indeed the Senator. He announced that the *Fired Up, Ready to Go* slogan was here to stay.

Everyone of us was on the edge of our seats including the ladies of Philomela. As we yearned for more, Edith patiently answered each question with energy and vigor as if it happened yesterday. The ladies kept firing question after question and Edith answered each one seemingly without tiring. I was amazed. I knew my cousin could do many things but never before had I seen her in action. Now the stage was set. Edith had been the inspiration behind a poem written by Myra Binns Bridgforth, and it had been set to music by Ian Coleman... a soloist.

Karen Lombardi Ingle recorded the piece and it was placed on CD by an employee with CNN. WOW! None of the Philomela ladies had ever met Edith before, yet her story had inspired them.

That same weekend, the ladies of Philomela were in concert at the Vienna, Baptist Church. For the first time, they sang the words to the poem entitled, "Change." It completely inspired Edith and I as we cried before the audience. How musical their voices sounded. They echoed harmoniously throughout the church. Yes, Edith S. Childs of Greenwood, South Carolina had been invited to Vienna, Virginia at the request of a small group of women who thought her story was inspiring.

As I listened to the accolades from the parishioners and visitors for my cousin, I was astonished to say the least. One hardly thinks of their own family being any more than just family, despite what they accomplish. However, on this weekend, a different light shone atop Edith. I came to view Edith far more than just a family member, but also as a lady with an inspiring voice. Once we were alone, we talked privately. And although we are family, I discovered a part of my cousin for the first time as a public figure that she has so honorably been for years. I was energized by it all.

At the end of the coral performance, Edith spoke to the congregation and ended with the _Fired Up Ready to Go_ chant which rang out in unison as if they were familiar with the chant used during the Civil Rights Movement. Setting all consideration aside, this was for the most part a Caucasian affair. Seemingly, in 2010, the chant has taken on a different and a more powerful meaning of hope that has encouraged people of varied backgrounds and nationalities to come closer together. I found myself changing as Edith recapped her encounter with Senator Obama. I noticed as she reiterated her story, persons in the congregation were totally engaged.

At the conclusion of the program, Edith greeted everyone with a smile and kind words. Although she had been standing for a long period of time, she remained steadfast. Many of the congregants just wanted to touch her just to have that degree of intimacy. She stayed on as long as there was a question unanswered.

I thought that I was politically savvy because I knew my Mayor, William D. Euille, City of Alexandria, VA, and my Congressman from Virginia 8th District, Jim Moran, Virginia Senator, Mark Warner and Governor Bob McDonnell. I had worked as an election official the past twelve-years. I worked the polls for various elections such as: presidential, governor, senator, councilman, school board just to name a few. I thought I was politically connected, but my cousin put my political savvies to shame with her campaigning and in-depth look at the issues.

Edith talked with people in various jurisdictions and attempted to meet their needs, such as: waterlines for rural families, establishing ride-share for senior citizens needing rides to medical appointments and organizing a back to school supply drive for students. Edith has been working for the people, who live in her district for many years. They know she can be counted on to do a job well done. She responds day or night if called upon.

I asked, "Why?"

She replied, "I know there is a need."

The 2008 presidential candidate she chose to endorse had to bring the same personal approach she was accustomed to giving her constituents.

Miranda Boozer

CHAPTER-TWENTY
After the Election

I was very happy after the election of 2008. It allowed me the opportunity to witness the inauguration of the nation's first black president that would be installed as elected leader the United States of America. My soul rejoiced over this long awaited day.

I had initially thought that I would be too old or even dead and not witness this day. The Lord's infinite wisdom made it possible for me and the world to experience this memorable occasion. The only thing that I requested from the Obama campaign were tickets to the inauguration celebration. In the past, I have supported candidates and received nothing in return after their elections. There were no thank you notes, phone calls or invitations.

Mrs. Wilhelmina Robinson, our group coordinator, made several attempts to book transportation to Washington. She contacted Boles Bus Lines and Henderson Bus Lines only to find that both were booked up. Through her perseverance, she was able book our group seats with an out of town bus line from Augusta, Georgia. Even though this bus line was well connected to the DC area, we were only able to make hotel room reservations in Williamsburg, PA. Our reservations took us to the Marriott Inn.

Our daughter, Jeannie and granddaughter, Lakeyia were on their way from Japan to celebrate with us in DC. They arrived Thursday before the inauguration. A long time family friend, Frank Starks, who lives in D.C., picked them up.

My tickets for the concert, inauguration, parade and the ball finally arrived. Our children were to be escorted to the concert and ball. Representative Anne Parks, flew to D.C. and delivered our children's invitations.

Monday, January 19, 2009, we were set to leave for Pennsylvania. About 4am, a reporter from WSPA TV-7 was knocking on my door asking for pictures. He followed us to Greenwood's Cross Creek Mall where we boarded the bus. Our driver, Jett was to escort us to Williamsburg. Williamsburg is two hours from Washington. We were finally on our way. The reporter rode with us as we sing *Fired Up Ready To Go*. There were a total of twenty-six people in our group. Jett stopped in Greenville to allow the reporter to get off.

During our trip, Jett stopped several time to allow the group to stretch our legs and purchase snacks. It was really a cold trip. Ice everywhere.

Ms. Melissa H. Murray made it possible for us to

adorn our own trademark tee-shirts. They were dark green with Greenwood, South Carolina aligning the top. *Fired Up Ready to Go* was also laid across the front bottom portion of the tee-shirt. Of course, we felt that we were special and really looking good. Bryan, a reporter from CBS, called me by cell to see what time we would arrive in D.C. I informed him that I would call when reach the stadium.

After our safe arrival, we gave thanks to God Almighty for watching over us during our journey. The bus pulled in to our destination late that evening. Our evening was well spent with dinner at the Merriot Restaurant. The young people played cards, watch movies and played other games. Frank picked up Charles at the bus terminal.

CBS's reporter Bryan met Lindaya and I in the parking lot. After approximately 5-6 buses picked up their passages, we boarded our bus, which was headed to the Washington Mall. We were only a mile from the Mall yet it took in excess of an hour and thirty minutes to get there. We stopped at 6th street.

We did not think that we were going to be observed. We had the instruction we needed to get in with our silver cards. The line wrapped around two building, which was about four or five blocks. Bryan said, "I will use my press badge to get us in."

Policemen were everywhere. When we finally arrived

at the press gate, Bryan stated, "They are with me."

That reminds me; it is not what you know but who you know, and fortunately this day we knew Bryan. The weather was very cool inauguration day. Everybody that were with us were wearing double everything just to keep warm. Some folk had been out all night in the cold weather just waiting for this event.

I could hardly believe that I was actually waiting for President Obama to be sworn in as the first black president. Aretha Franklin sang *God Bless America*. She sings with so much poise. And to mention hat and her coat was beautiful. One knows that I was looking at her headgear.

President Obama gave his heart warming speech. I was inspired. He stated, "This is neither a blue nor a red state, this is the United States of an America." And with his right hand raised high, he took the oath. Tears poured down my face. These were truly tears of joy in witnessing this grand occasion.

Indeed, this will become a story to tell my great-grand children. I will forever treasure this occasion. I reminisce sometimes about this great day, and I still get goose bumps all over.

Listed below are the members that were in our group that traveled to Washington, DC to witness President Barack Obama's installment:

Charles Childs, Edith Childs, our grand-daugther, Lindaya Brown, Clara Sheppard, Ann Gunby, Margarett Gainey, Lillian Thomas, Ruth Forrest, Earlean Boles, Kay Owens, Melissa Hawkins, Steve Murray, Bernetta Baylor, Mary Warren, Cynthia Warren, Betty Boles, Wilhelemia Robinson, Mary H. Williams, Doris Johnson, Marian Gary, Rosa Marshall, Deon Kelly, Bobbie Crawford, Ms. Burton, Kyle (a Lander College student) and Jett (our driver). We had a safe trip to Washington and a safe return.

Nov.23, 2009 I received an invitation to the holiday reception at the White House to be held Dec.4th at 6pm.

This was awesome experience. I had never been inside the White House before. Of course, I gladly accepted the invitation. My cousin, Miranda Boozer were cleared for the event with our social security number, address and date of birth. It was an honor to see President Obama and Mrs. Obama again.

Miranda and I exited the VIP room to greet President Obama and the First Lady. Incredibly, the response from President Obama was, "Do y'all know who this is? Do y'all know who this is? This Edith Childs, my *Fired up Ready to Go* lady from Greenwood, SC. He continued smiling.

Mrs. Obama stated, "Edith, you have made his day. We are so happy you came."

The President then asked, "How was everyone doing in Greenwood?"

Smiling, I responded, "Everyone sends their love to you and Mrs. Obama, Mr. President."

"Tell them I love them back," he replied.

There were people from all over the US. I met people from Texas, Iowa, NH, Colorado, NM. Delaware. Fla. NY, to just name a few places. And to think, little ole Edith S. Childs was among the crowd.

Dec, 14th, 2010, Miranda and I gladly accept a second invitation to the White House. Again, I was honored to be on the guest list. This is the message I wrote on my VIP card *Fired Up Ready to Move On* to get the job done. Thank you Mr. President for what you are doing to make a difference in our lives. Frankly speaking, anytime I am invited to the White House, I will be on my way in a flash. I will hurriedly reserve reservations (via) the Amtrak for Charles and I.

I give many thanks to David Agnew and Jason Green for their joint agreements and permissions granted me during the compilation of my book.

My first White House visit.

Edith arrives at the
White House gates.

White House lights at night.

Edith and Miranda relaxing
while visiting the White House.

Edith poses with Laurie, White
House staff.

Edith and Miranda poses
in the White House Library.

Edith and Marinda poses for a
picture in front of the White House
Christmas Tree-(the Green Room).

Edith poses with Bo, the First Family's pet at the White House.

Whites House staff serving during holiday reception.

The 44th President Barack Obama at the White House.

First Lady, Mrs. Michelle Obama at the White House.

Miranda and Edith stands beside the White House decrative cake.

Edith has a cause to celebrate after the election and Inauguration of the 44th President Barack Obama.

CHAPTER-TWENTY ONE
What We Think About Edith S. Childs
Unforgettable Experiences

Our family has known Edith Sanders Childs since she was in high school. She is a very courageous and an out going lady. Edith is one that can wear many hats, whether it is spiritual or secular.

Mrs. Childs is one who has a true love for mankind, always putting the needs of others before herself and willing to help out in any way that she can.

Greenwood has been blessed to have Edith as a part of this community. She has truly been as asset on the state, local and national levels.

We love you Edith and may the Almighty God continue to bless you richly in all of your endeavors.

The Obbie Tolbert Family

When we think about Edith Childs we think about Micah 6:8 (KJV). She exemplifies this scripture by her life. *He hath shewed thee, O man, what is good; and what doth the Lord require of thee, but to do justly, and to love mercy, and to walk humbly with thy God?*

God requires that we do what is right and fair in our relationships with other people. Sister Childs has a sense of standards of equality among all people. It can be said that she is honest in even the smallest routine business transaction.

Her heart is filled with compassion and kindness toward others. But what I Love the most is her humility. She is not arrogant at all even through all that God has blessed her with... she remains humble. That is why we believe God has chosen her to serve his people.

Reverend and Mrs. Archie Fair

April 15, 2009, I invited Edith Childs to speak to our United Methodist Men's group. I knew that her visit would be a special occasion. For one thing, she was well-known to our members because the town of Troy is in the area of Greenwood County for which she is the representative on the County Council. For another, her energetic concerns for all people in her district came across in her public appearances and official statements. Moreover, she had originated a presidential campaign slogan for the Senator Barack Obama when he appeared at Lander University: *Fired Up and Ready to Go.*

Even so, I was impressed even more so when Edith and her husband, Charles appeared that evening at the Fellowship Hall of Troy United Methodist Church. They were in the company of two additional people, a reporter and a photographer, but they were not from the Greenwood Index Journal. They were with the Washington Post.

They were in the process of conducting an in-depth interview for a front-page article about Greenwood, which was to be printed Sunday, April 26. Teasingly, I told Edith that I had been unaware that she traveled with her personal corps.

Edith's conversation with our group during that occasion, and from the content of the Post article, I learned how perceptive and compassionate she really is. Edith represents her constituency and addresses their needs. As a former college instructor of public speaking, I immediately appreciated her delightfully self-effacing humor and her articulate analysis of pertinent issues. She is simply delightful to listen to.

When the Washington Post article appeared, one of the editors, who had been a friend of my sons at Greenwood High, sent me a copy of the issue. There on the front page was a picture of Edith with my wife and me. That really got me *Fired Up and Ready To Go!*

Dr. N. Keith Polk

Sister Edith, you exemplify God through your life of caring for others. *For even the Son of man came not to be ministered unto, but to minister, and to give his life a ransom for many* Mark 10:45 (KJV). You are tireless in all that you do for your fellow man. And to God be the glory for the mighty things He is doing through you.

Reverend Joseph Caldwell
Pastor Crossroad Baptist Church

I have known Edith Childs since high school. Edith has always been vocal, inspirational and a people person. She has served in public office for years. Her passion has always been helping and assisting. Mrs. Childs retired as a nurse and continued her public work as a member of Greenwood County Council. I live in a small Black community so named *Promise Land*. While I was attending Lander University in Greenwood, the class was asked to write a paper on their community.

Dr. Beth Bethel, our professor, was interested in my account on how *Promise Land* community got its name. My account was that it was relative to racial injustice. Blacks was promised a certain amount of property but never received it. While Mrs. Childs was a member of the County Council, she was instrumental in the county passing legislation to install traffic lights in the heart of two busy crossings.

She has also done tremendous work in negotiation efforts to convince local landowners to allow an exit road across their property if the train blocked the only exit, if an emergency vehicle was needed.

Not only was Mrs. Childs concerned for her county council duties, she was constantly aware of the need to be actively involved with the youth. For many years she has organized Back to School events for the youth. Mrs. Childs is notorious for wearing fancy hats. My wife has made hats that Mrs. Childs has often admired.

Reverend and Mrs. Bernard White

I met Mrs. Childs about eighteen-years-ago at a church function. Mrs. Childs is a strong community leader that is always willing to lend a helping hand. Edith is always doing for the youth and supporting our schools and school leaders. I admire Mrs. Childs and how she supports many church functions in the surrounding area. She is always putting others before herself. I am very appreciative that Edith is a part of my life and community.

Venise L. Bolden

I have known Edith for many years. For that reason, I can say that she is fired up and ready to go. Edith has proven herself to be a servant with high standards. She gives her best to whatever she sets out to accomplish. She honestly loves people because she denies herself at times, and she focuses on what she can do for her community, state and her country. Edith's service does not stop in just Greenwood alone. It is too difficult to say all of what I think of Edith in just a few words, other than that she is caring, considerate, focused, and she wants to her best for everyone.

Calvin D. Simpkins, Sr.

Edith is committed and willing in causes above and beyond. She is truly fired up and ready to go. She truly serves God through her service rendered for the people. God is so good, even to me.

Gwen Wiggleton

Edith is a class act, a rare find, humble, and she is honest. She is always worried and concerned about the health and welfare of others, in whatever way she can be of help 24/7. She is faithful, loyal and a true friend.

Mary W. Greene

Mrs. Childs is a woman of faith, a faithful wife and mother. We have known her for many years. Her hard work and caring spirit have impacted the lives of many from serving on the school board to being elected to serve as our County Councilwoman. Edith has led the way in bringing change to Greenwood for the better. She is a breath of fresh air and has a heart of gold, especially when she sees the needs of others.

Pastor Bobby and Rose Childs
Youth Crusade Evangelistic Center

Edith is a unique person. She does kind deeds. She gives love unselfishly. She expects no payment and no words of praise when she helps people. I have found Edith to be a dear friend. She is there for me in good and bad times. She is a friend that I can count on to be at my side. Edith is a person who strives for doing her best. She is always working to better her community.

As you begin to know Edith, you will find that she is as sentimental and as soft as can be. Edith is always *Fired Up and Ready to Go*. She gives so much, but asks for little. Edith is a people person.

Ojetter Williams

"The Most Important Job"

Good afternoon, as the father of two young daughters, I know that being a father is one of the most important jobs any man can have.

My own father left my family when I was two-years-old. I was raised by a heroic mother and wonderful grandparents who provided the support, discipline and love that helped me get to where I am today, but I still felt the weight of that absence throughout my childhood. It's something that leaves a hole no government can full. Studies show that children who grow up without their fathers around are more likely to drop out of high school, goo to hail, or become teen fathers themselves.

And while no government program can fill the role that fathers play for our children, what we can do is try to support fathers who are willing to step up and fulfill their responsibly as parents, partners and providers. That's why last year I started a nationwide dialogue on fatherhood to tackle the challenge of father absence head on.

In Chicago, the Department of Health and Human Services held a forum with community leaders, fatherhood experts and everyday dads to discuss the importance of responsible fatherhood support programs. In New Hampshire, Secretary of Education Duncan explored the linkages between father absence and educational attainment in children. In Atlanta, Attorney General Holder spoke with fathers in the criminal justice system about ways local reentry organizations, domestic violence groups and fatherhood programs can join together to support ex-offenders and incarcerated individuals who want to be closer to their families and children.

Now we are taking this to the next level. Tomorrow, I'll make an announcement about the next phase of our efforts to help fathers fulfill their responsibilities as parents. You can learn more at: www.fatherhood.gov.

This Father's Day—I'm thankful for the opportunity to be a dad to two wonderful daughters. And I'm thankful for all the wonderful fathers, grandfathers, uncles, brothers and friends, who are doing their best to make a difference in the lives of a child.

Barack Obama
President of the United States of America

My friend, Edith S. Childs is such a wonderful person. She is the most caring, loving, smartest and the sweetest woman I know. She's my source of courage when trouble comes my way. Edith takes time out to listen and understand. She has been a great inspiration in my life, and she's such a godly woman with wisdom of God's ways. Edith has always been a leader and never a follower. She loves to help others; she has a heart full of love. I wish there were more on earth like my friend. Friends are so hard to find; Edith S. Childs is one of a kind.

Effie M. White

Edith is a woman of many hats. Over the years, Edith has been a hardworking person in this community. As a councilwoman she has always been driven, motivated and determined to make a difference. Councilwoman Edith Childs has always stood firm and supportive in the county, the state and all the way to the White House. She has proven that leadership is a journey and not a quick trip.

Willie and Paulette Randall

Edith has been a friend to our family for as long I can remember. She will do whatever she can for anyone. Her love for people makes all the difference in our community. We think God for her.

James and Barbara Martin

I have known Mrs. Edith Childs for quite a while. Her husband, Charles and I were classmates in school. Edith (as I lovingly call her) is a person with a vision and a goal. She never let anything or anyone stop her from reaching for the stars. She is truly a "go-getter" and does what she has to do with integrity. Edith believes in rightness for all mankind. If she tells you something, you can bank on it. My wife was not driven when we picked up one of our local papers here in Wilmington and saw pictures of Edith dancing with the President of the United States. We knew one day it would happen that she would be in the White House with the President. Edith we say to you, continue to let God order your steps because He is not through with you yet.

Lovota and Carolyn

As a child of God, Edith shares a common heritage of divine love with all people. As she interacts, agree or disagree with other's points of view, she appreciates the diversity that adds richness, beauty and strength to the tapestry of humankind. She recognizes the interconnectedness of all human beings and trusts that every situation and person has the potential to contribute to life in a positive way. Therefore, she maintains an attitude of gratitude and positive thinking wherein she speaks only positive words and affirmations, even when appearances indicate the opposite. Where there is a difference of opinion, she looks beyond the seeming boundaries of the disagreement to find common ground.

Edith is a strong advocate of family values, education, loyalty, honesty, integrity and respect. Continuously, she goes out of her way to provide the needy by feeding the hungry and clothing the naked. Her service to the community and surrounding areas is the epitome of *What Would Jesus do.*

It is not very common to find someone who will deny their wants and needs to help others, especially when you are criticized and sometime feel unappreciated. Through it all, Edith keeps the right perspective and maintains a positive state of being. Even in the face of difficult circumstances, her spirit does not fail. This in no way discourages Edith from rendering services to so many people in her loving ways.

Without a doubt, Edith is a true servant to mankind. I humbly express my thanks for selflessly giving her time and talents.

Barbara B. Tompkins

Edith shows spunk and devotion when she is trying to make things happen. I have great admiration for her in that regard. She is a *mover and shaker.*

I have often wondered about the part she played in out last presidential election. Her *Fired up and Ready to Go* chant became a rallying cry for Obama. Indeed one little lady from Greenwood, South Carolina did play a successful role in Barack Obama becoming President of the United States. That's powerful! Who would believe what one voice could do?

I presently find that Edith and I have similar interest in working together to make Greenwood a richer more congenial community. There is a placard in my puppet place that says, "All caring people join hands together to uplift the world." So now, Edith, if you will let me join hands with you, would be so honored.

Suzy Holloway

I must start off on a personal not about Mrs. Childs. She has been a friend since first meeting her. She has a warm and caring spirit that is a gift from God, and she carries it with her wherever she goes. She's a person of character, honesty and always tells it like it is, and of course, her laughter tops it all.

Mrs. Childs is a religious God fearing woman working in the church and always willing to help and serve. I first learned about Mrs. Childs through my mother, the late Mrs. Rachel White, who had told me how devoted Mrs. Childs was to the community.

Being a activist, I am originally from Chicago. I did not know the procedures on how to get started with a cleanup project for my neighborhood. I talked to my mother, who suggested that I contact Mrs. Childs. On meeting Mrs. Childs, she made everything much easier, not only did she give me the information I needed, she showed up on the day of the community project and rendered her services. Since that time, she has become a friend as well as someone I highly respect as great leader in the community.

We also worked together in the Health Ministry in churches and the community to teach and promote healthy living styles.

As our County Councilwoman, she has fulfilled her duties, and she has made a great impact in our community by serving everyone. Some of her duties go outside of her position, such as planning events for food drives, health ministry and holiday events for children and adults giving gifts as well.

Last but not least, Edith had a very positive affect on President Obama during his visit to Greenwood with Fired Up and Ready to Go. Let's not forget she is also called the hat lady because she loves her hats.

Mrs. Mary E. Smith

Mrs. Edith Childs is awesome in every sense of the word. She has such a caring heart for everyone she comes into contact with. She is a go-getter and does not procrastinate on important issues. She's the most unselfish person we know. She often stand alone in tackling some of the most controversial issues. We admire her on so many levels. And oh, can she wear those hats!

Reverend John
and Elnita Williams

As we reflect back on the many years we have known Edith, she has been a mover and shaker politically and culturally in Greenwood. Her main aspirations have been to help others to become rich with knowledge about many situations, helping people help themselves and working on their behalf to get things done to make their lives better. Her work in Morris Chapel Baptist Church, and many other clubs and organizations have given her the ability to reach people much farther than her Greenwood roots.

Whenever called upon, Edith is always willing to share and do her best to ensure the situation is resolved timely. She shares information that is based on her personal experiences. She illustrates how life's hardships can become life lessons that teach us how to grow, heal and love. She tells her audiences that the pains of yesteryear are not necessarily life's reality.

People that Edith has met along the way from the County Court House, the State House, and the White House remember her for her diligence, her love for people, her creative talents and her beautiful hats and her trust in God. We are certain that she realizes she could not have accomplished anything without her best friend and husband, Charles, who gave her much encouragement, support and love.

We are supportive of what she is doing and all that we know she will continue to do. We are proud of her accomplishments, knowing that all the help she received along the way would be used in her life. We feel humble and grateful that such a human being is a part our lives.

We hope this book will encourage you to search your soul and make some long range plans about where you want to go. In closing, we would like to share a citation by John Wesley:

> Do all the good you can,
> By all the means you can
> In all the ways you can,
> In all the places you can,
> At all the times you can,
> To all the people you can,
> As long as ever you can"

May God continue to shower His many blessings upon you and give you peace. Always remember success I knowing that one other human being has breathed easier because you have lived.

Donald & Jean Robinson
children *Michelle Donna,*
Sabrina and their families

Edith is one of the most accomplished women I have met. She literally, wears many hats in the community, the church and the State of South Carolina. I'm proud to call her my adopted sister. She has the characteristics of a true Christian woman showing concern for everyone in the district she represents as well as the other districts. She is very loving and is a caring person, who goes the extra mile to help where it is needed. It seems she never gets tire of doing good for others.

Edith has functioned continuously for a number of years in that position. Her steadfastness in working for the common good has carried her many places, including the White House where she was a guest of the President of the United States, Barack Obama and First Lady Michelle Obama. Whether it is appearing on television in the national news, visiting Japan, or hosting a Town Meeting in the community, she remains humble and acknowledging her blessings from the Lord.

Edith and Charles is a loving couple with children and grandchildren. She is not only a virtuous woman, but also a fashionable woman. She is noted for her beautiful hats to fit all occasions and for her impeccable and elegant wardrobe. I am proud to be her sister and one of her fashion coordinators. Congratulations Edith, on being a phenomenal.

Bernice Evans Norman
Owner of Bern's Clothing

I'm going to tell you a little story of how I met Mrs. Edith Childs. My niece was Mrs. Child's hairstylist for years. My niece became ill and couldn't do Mrs. Childs hair anymore. I met Mrs. Childs in 2007; I started taking care of her hair in my niece's place in my salon Pat's House of Beauty.

Mrs. Childs is an inspiration to everyone. I can ask her anything about life; she always gives me correct advice. I talked with her about personal matters that I cannot speak with my family about and it doesn't go any further. She just offers professional advice.

Mrs. Childs is caring to my family and me. She always asks about my ill niece. You can always count on her for anything. She is a motivational speaker. When asked to speak anywhere, Mrs. Childs always tells me to love my true self; believe in myself; do not allow anyone to tell me that I cannot do it. Doing what you love may change and save your life. When you find your passion, operate out o f your passion. Having a large income doesn't matter when it comes to God. God will provide, produce and protect you while you are pursuing your passion.

I have met many women in my life, some have inspired me and some have encouraged me with their faith and some have impressed me with their life. I can say that Mrs. Childs has truly inspired me deeply. She is a godly woman who is kind, eager, fixed in her love for God.

Mrs. Childs is a remarkable woman.

Patricia Jones-Yeldell

In 2000, I came to meet Mrs. Childs. She had been elected to District One's seat on the County Council. I do not remember our first encounter but I am sure it was an enjoyable one based on all visits I have had with her. She is a delightful person to be around, always with a smile and the words, *How Can I help.*

In 2001, the City of Troy had applied through Upper Savannah Council of Government for a CDBG grant to install water lines in Troy and surrounding areas. Mrs. Childs was instrumental in helping Troy secure matching funds from Greenwood and McCormick Counties. With this and a commitment from Mike Gulledge's office, the grant was awarded. McCormick County agreed to extend their lines into the Troy area. For the first time, other than the town's well, Troy now has city water.

In 2007, Mrs. Childs called me and stated, "Get me some estimates for a new fire truck."

At the town meeting, in September 2006, she had asked, "What does Troy need?"

"Waterline extensions or another fire truck would better serve the public," was the reply she received.

Mrs. Childs was successful in getting Greenwood County Council to approve funds for the fire truck. It was finally ordered with a price tag of $238,000.

I have always found Mrs. Childs ready and willing to help in any way that she can. Edith has obtained funds to assist the summer programs for the kids in her district and Troy was well to attended and enjoyed by the young people. I admire Mrs. Childs for her loyalty to her people in District 1 and to the County of Greenwood. She is a very likable person, friendly an always willing to find answers. She is famously known as the *HAT LADY*, she is *Fired Up and Ready to Go*. Thank you for all that you have done for the people of Troy and most of all for your friendship.

Mayor Jimmy Peeler
Town of Troy, SC

Edith Childs was born in modest circumstances. She is an encouragement to those who think they cannot make it. Her life is a testimony that you do not have to stay where life drops you. Something within Edith found infinite insight at the intersection where life dropped her and the purpose for which God made her. We give thanks to God Almighty for the mighty things that He has done through her many expressions of ministry and civic duties through the years. She has been a strong and positive role model and an example to many. She has been busy keeping her finger on the fast forward button in Greenwood. Edith is a walking example of our Lord's challenge to be *Faithful over a few things and I will make you ruler over much.*

Edith Childs is a people person. If someone has a need she is there. She is a resourceful person. If you have a resource that can be utilized by someone in the community, she will contact you. She is known nationwide as the *Hat Lady* from Greenwood. More importantly, she is known by what is under her hat—a mind to do what needs to be done for the people of Greenwood County.

Edith stretches her wings to rise to the level where God wants her. Edith was made to soar.

Dr. Willie S. Harrison
Reverend Sandra W. Harrison

An inquisitive child, Edith was destined to make a difference in life. Often "shee-ed" in school for asking why and wanting to know the reason(s), Edith was sometimes mislabeled as a busybody. Possessing this persistent personality, she convinced her classmates to ask questions about life. This little, yet significant, footnote about Edith's childhood, is presently a subject of many jokes.

Perhaps, a more challenging undertaking was growing up in an unjust society. She encountered a Klu Klux Klan march; they were draped in white sheets and carried torches.

There were many positive experiences along the way to adulthood also. First, Edith was blessed to be reared in a Christian home and to appreciate church going.

Along the way, Edith met her husband Charles, who is and has been very supportive and caring for nearly four decades. Also along the way, Edith acquired a passion for helping others beyond her career of nursing. She entered the political arena with an attitude that she didn't know everything, but she was willing to listen to people and make their needs and wants known. Edith does not sit back and always wait for people to come to her, she looks for and pursues ways to help improve life individually and on a community wide basis.

I have never heard Edith complain for herself, it is always about the needs and desires of other people. Under perplexing conditions, she always encouraging to let's do what we can do even if it does not appear to be a lot. Edith is known and accepted throughout the community well enough to be referred to by her first name only, Edith, and people will know whom you are talking about.

For a person born in her circumstances it was a great privilege to be called upon by the President of the United States. As a result she has been inundated with calls from all over the nation seeking her advice. Edith has beaten the odds.

Dr. R. C. Moore,
Educator

Blessings are God's gifts to us. He has blessed every person with some gift or ability, bringing glory to His name. They can be simple or great. Some are obvious and shine brightly in front of everyone, while others move about unnoticed. He has blessed you with the awesome gift of giving and serving others as a beacon in the night. It is our prayer that as you continue to use your gifts to bless and to serve, you will continue to be blessed, also.

"Let your light so shine before men, that they may see your good works, and glorify your Father which is in heaven" (Matthew 5:16).

Blanton and Anita Smith

I have known County Councilwoman Edith Childs for a number of years. She is one that you can call on. She believes in getting things done. She is trustworthy, honest, responsible and dependable.

Mrs. Childs is a woman of integrity and a leader to all humankind regardless of race, gender or religion and she demonstrates it daily by serving her community, her church and in the political arena.

Randy Jackson

Mrs. Edith Childs: A servant of people, I came to know her after I was elected to the Greenwood County Council. Up until that time, I knew who she was but never had the opportunity to know her personally. It did not take me long to realize that Mrs. Childs stood out from the other members of the council. She was a woman on the council and is the only member who can embellish a room with a hat.

I soon found out that Mrs. Childs distinguished herself in another way that is through her tireless and dedicated service to the people of Greenwood County. She consistently is a champion of the less fortunate and regularly challenges other members of council to be motivated. Jesus admonished his followers not to forget the less fortunate. He even said that when you help those in need, you are I indeed serving him. In public office and private, Edith embodies that spirit of service. And I admire and respect her for that.

Dr. & Mrs. Chuck Moates

Edith Childs is a woman who wears many beautiful hats. But there is so much more to her than what she wears on her head. She has a number of talents and abilities that she uses to improve the community and live of so many others. Whether she is helping to organize a Back to School Bash or helping to elect the President of the United States. She is *Fired Up and Ready to GO!*

Reverend and Mrs. Clyde D. Cannon

I met Edith Childs in 1997 while I served on the Greenwood County Council. I did not choose to seek the council seat again. Therefore, Edith was elected to run for County Council District one. She came to every council meeting prior to being sworn in to her seat on the council.

Edith always has displayed a willingness to assist the people of her district. You will find her at community meetings, greeting people with that great big smile. Her smile turns into determination and resolve when she is trying to push the council to agree with her on a cause, she feels strongly about. Edith is quick to ask for advice from the people in her district on matters that concern her district. Edith has shown a concern for my family over the years and has shown a sincere concern for their well being.

It is a known fact, that if Edith expresses her opinion about a matter, her opinion will be the same next week and the weeks thereafter. I describe her as a strong oak tree planted firmly that is not pushed around by every little wind that blows her direction. When Edith gets *Fired Up and ready to Go* about a project in the community, you can bet that she will be successful in her endeavors in completing the project.

I am proud to call Edith Childs, my friend. I wish all the politicians had her character and determination to do what is best for the citizens.

D. Ansel Brewer
President, Greenwood Financial Service, Inc.
Owner, Brewer Enterprises
Former County Council Member #1

Mrs. Edith Childs has been a friend of the family for years. I find her to be caring and a kind person to all she meets. It is my prayer we will have more Edith's in the world.

Reverend Oscar Klugh

Tribute to Edith Childs
A Force within our Community and Beyond

There are many words to describe Edith Childs. Each word is positive. This tireless driven woman is first and foremost a woman of her word. Within her smiling eyes shine the intensity of a fighter, the compassion of a nurturing care giver, the tenacity of a winner, the concern of a genuine motivator and a champion of the human spirit. All of these qualities are wrapped up in one who is just as comfortable with the homeless as she is with the leader of the free world, the President of the United States of America.

Edith wears many hats, accomplishes many worthwhile tasks, and always remains ready to assist whenever and wherever she is needed. Her presence is jovial and cannot be denied, because when Edith Childs walks into a room, everyone is pleasantly impacted by her confidence and grace. She holds herself and others, accountable. She has a way of bringing out the highest level of capabilities in those that she encounters. Consistency of spirit and action describe Edith Childs.

Within the community, she has served faithfully as a school board member of the Greenwood School District 50. She kept the best interests of the children of Greenwood School District 50 in mind at all times, while serving in full capacity as an active school board member. Under her watch, she assured that sensible decisions were being made for the good of children, parents, and the community. She continued and expanded her community impact through her decision to run for a seat on the Greenwood County Council for District One. Through a positive, encompassing campaign, Edith won the hearts and votes of her constituents, and has never let them down. She seeks and finds answers to problems in the community such as homelessness, crime, hunger, safe drinking water, and secures countless other resolutions which improve our community. Edith is a constant supporter of education and a servant and motivator to the children in Greenwood County through various activities such as the annual Back to School Bash, frequents classrooms motivational speaking engagements, and special annual holiday giving events where families are provided a nourishing meal and gifts for the children in the household. Loving kindness describes Edith Childs.

Beyond the local community, Edith Childs can be credited for spurring a nation into action with the famous chant *Fired Up, Ready to Go*. These words and her unwillingness to embrace the status quo thinking of the past, drove an entire nation to move forward and believe that yes we can. Not one to look for recognition for deeds done, Edith received and accepted one of the highest honors a citizen can receive—a personal invitation from President Obama and First Lady, Michelle Obama. Edith Childs is a person who is not only guided from within, but also from the early words of her grandmother who told her at a very young age that she was going to be somebody some day. She holds those words deep in her heart. Edith is wise, therefore, she knows the power of motivating words. Strong and determined describe Edith Childs.

In her faith, Edith Childs has shown herself to be one who is not daunted by the troubles in life. She is not exempt from the snares and disappointments that come in a lifetime. She does, however, demonstrate through her life that we all must walk by faith, not by sight. She shows all of us how to radiate grace under fire and how to keep looking up amidst trials. She is a committed member of Morris Chapel Baptist Church, but is a welcome visitor to many local churches. Edith Childs has never met a stranger and actively practices the Golden Rule.

Edith Childs is a force within our community and beyond.

Williams, Sandra
Taylor, and Teresa Watson

Our family has a rich history, and as a family, we have broken through some of the barriers in life. As a person of great influence in our family, my Aunt Edith S. Childs has made an impact on our family, the city of Greenwood, the state and National level as well. As the first known Pastor, Preacher and Author in the family, I am so honored to know that my Aunt is doing great things for the Lord, the nation and the world. I am so proud of her and the many accomplishments that are associated with her name and reputation. As a woman of faith, she holds conversations with God on a daily basis and truly awaits His guidance and directions.

Edith depicts a love for people and a strong desire to serve at all levels. She possess a faith that is truly commendable. If I had to take three words to describe her, they would be as follows; nurturer, motivator, and cheerleader have no voice and yet giving them a voice to say what needs to be said. She cheers the loudest for what is right and push easily with the spirit of excellence.

I just want to personally and publicly thank you for your love and the wisdom you have shared with me over the years. I remember when you took me to Pizza Hut when I was a young boy to teach me table etiquette and mannerism, a lesson I will never forget. Thank you for all that you do and not only for me, our family, but also for the nation. You are a living legend and a national icon in my book. Keep the faith and always keep your eyes on Christ Jesus; He will never leave you nor forsake you.

As a motivator, Edith moves a crow from a calm to a roaring sea of believers. My aunt can motivate the most unmotivated person to achieving the goals and dreams through lifting their spirits and opening their minds to think that they can do great things. Her team building attainments has caused communities to rise to a common goal for all of humanity.

As a nurturer, she provides assistance to those who are in need, through her constant giving of food, clothes, school supplies, with transportation as well as with career development. My aunt is a cheerleader for people, as she looks out for those who have no voice, and yet she gives them a voice to say what needs to be said. She cheers the loudest for what is right and pushes with ease and a spirit of excellence.

I just want to personally and publicly thank you for your love and the wisdom you have shared with me over the years. I remember when you took me to Pizza hunt when I was a young boy to teach me table etiquette and mannerism, a lesson I will never forget. Thank you for all that you do and not only for me, our family, but also for the nation.

You are a living legend and a national icon in my book. Keep the faith and always keep your eyes on Christ Jesus, He will never leave you nor forsake you.

Reverend Anthony Sanders

I have known Mrs. Edith Childs more than thirty years

years. She does not mind going that extra mile to provide services wherever needed in her community.

Mrs. Childs is a true Christian; she attends Morris Chapel Baptist Church in Greenwood S C. I would like to describe her as a very hard worker, and she is a team player, who all could reliably count on. She is committed to her family, church and community. She has a good heart. Mrs. Childs is willing to help in any way she can. She is trustworthy, and she is a pleasure to have as a friend.

Mrs. Childs believes in herself, gives of her time, finances and always volunteers to help others in need.

Earlean W. Boles

I have had the pleasure of knowing Councilwoman Edith Childs for more than twenty-five-years. She is honest, trustworthy and a very responsible person. She willingly gives of her service and talents for the improvement of mankind. She is and has always been a proud black woman with impeccable strength. She makes a conscious effort to do well by those who are less fortunate and especially those who are of the household of faith. She enjoys giving, and expecting nothing in return. Her tireless labor and attainments are well respected by the Promised Land Community. It warms her spirit and brings joy to her heart when she is able to make a difference in lives of others.

Edith's commitment to God, her family, friends and mankind as a whole are reasons why her living is not in vain.

Linda Cason

Integrity, extreme dedication, and an ongoing willingness to serve, are words that define Council Woman, Edith Childs. Her gentle demeanor and diminutive stature contradict the powerhouse of vision and experience that reside within, but these characteristics become evident when reviewing her remarkable involvement in local government and community service.

A synonym for Edith is *compassion.* She is involved in many programs involving preparing kids for school and feeding those less fortunate. Childs has been co-sponsoring Thanksgiving and Christmas dinners for the needy for the last decade.

The Bible defines the meaning of compassion in several ways. *We are to speak for those who cannot speak for themselves, and defend the rights of the poor* (Proverbs 31:8-9, NM). We do this by taking action instead of just talking about helping others: *tear children, let us not love with words or tongue but with actions and in truth"* (1 John 3:18, NW).

Councilwoman Edith Childs is a replication of God's

inspirational compassion.

She is truly an overwhelming blessing to the city...
Greenwood.

Reverend Curtis and Carolyn Carter

Edith Childs is a visionary who takes on gainsays with
the desire to win. She's a hard, dedicated worker truly
concerned about her community. Mrs. Childs is one of
the pillars of the Greenwood community. She keeps
the people in Greenwood within and outside of her
district informed on the many political issues that will
affect them in a positive or negative way.

Edith helps our people to understand the complicated
amendments that are to be voted on during election
times so they can vote with full knowledge of what
they, are voting for. She is a champion for human
rights no matter the race, gender or ethnic
background.

Mrs. Childs has a strong background in the health care
field and is always sponsoring events In the
community to help raise the awareness of her race on
the many health care challenges that we face. She has
a hat for the youth of our community in that she
sponsors events like a Back to School Bash to help
equip them with the tools and materials needed to be
successful in school. I can personally say that Mrs.

Childs is a loving treat who is able to connect in a positive way with the people that she leads. Thank God that she is in the Greenwood community. I truly believe that all of our lives are better and have been enriched because of her strong family values, spirituality, and firm leadership.

Pastor Jerry Brown

Edith started at a young age unselfishly fighting for equal rights. She is recognized nationally, having ties with President Obama... *Fired Up, Ready to Go!*

Bernice Warren Rhinehart

We have known Ms. Edith Childs for well more than thirty-years. We have interacted with her through a number of activities, such as church, community, civic, governmental and many others ventures. Our children grew up together while also attending school together.

Ms. Childs has always been very involved in the community, trying to make a positive difference for all of our citizens. If we had more role models like her, our nation would be a better place.

Steve & Lou Amye Odom

Mrs. Edith Childs is a very good person. She always does what she says she is going to do. She is a very outstanding woman. We love her.

George & Annette Carter

Edith Childs has been a true friend over twenty-five-years. Her belief has always been that you must look after your community and friends for any town to be successful. She always stand behind her convictions, constituents and community and for that the citizens of Greenwood are truly blessed.

Bal Ballentine

Congratulations on your first book. Thank you for sharing the intimacies of your life with us. Thank you for all of your hard work, time and commitments in making things happen. We give thanks and praise to God for the many contributions you've made to our communities and churches. May God continue to bless and use you in His Will.

Reverend Kenneth and
Sister Cynthia Harrison

In 1964, I became friends with Edith Sanders, after she began dating one of my friends. I knew her before then from Brewer High School's campus.

In 1965, Edith had a daughter named Linda. I would stop by her house from time to time and talk to her and see the baby.

In 1966, I was drafted into the United States Army. I lost contact with Edith for a long time. In fact, I was unaware that she was married or even a member of Greenwood's County Council. I have not lived in the Hodges or the Greenwood area since 1966.

Edith is the type of person you do not have to see or talk with every day to retain a friendship. However, I did see Edith and her family during the Inauguration of President Obama, and again the following July in Washington, D.C. I am very proud of Edith for all the things she has accomplished. Now, I read the Index Journal via the Internet to keep up with her.

Frank Starks

Edith is always *Fired Up and Ready to Go* in all that she does. Wherever the road leads her, rather it's to feed the hungry, visit the sick and shut in, on special occasions, birthday parties or retirement dinners.

Edith has severed on the Greenwood County Council in District-One for many years. Whenever there a need in our community, you can call on her. Edith will be there, and if she cannot work it out, she will find someone who can and she will not give up until it is done.

Edith has demonstrated that she is a child of God. She lets her light shine in all her work. Edith, you and Charles keep up the good work, you will received your just reward in heaven at the end of your journey.

E is for enthusiastic
D is for devoted
I is for intelligent
T is for thoughtfulness
H is for heartfelt feelings

Willie and Gladys Anderson

To my little sister whom I love dearly; she is such an inspiration to our family and the community. She has a big heart, open arms and willingness to do and help anyone she can. Edith is a Christian. She always puts God first in her life. You can call her anytime.

She loves feeding and clothing those in need. Above all, she is devoted to her family and friends. Edith is a retired practical nurse. She has been a strong caring and loving care giver for our entire family including our sister, mother, brothers and our aunt. My God has blessed her to reach many goals, dreams and aims in life.

Marie Jefferson

Edith is a very caring and loving person. She is a friend to everyone regardless of your situation or status in society. Over the years of knowing her, I have seen her love for helping people transform into a passion. She has always shown traits of leadership. I speak from experience when I say that she has always been there no matter what the situation. She always helps you to solve a problem, or she puts you on the right road to getting the problem solved.

Edith never places you on hold, and if she is not home to answer a call, she would always give you a return call. She is a God fearing woman, who is truly aware of The Ten Commandments that God left behind as our guide.

Edith goes the extra mile in everything she does, no matter what organization she is representing. My family is truly blessed to know Mrs. Edith Childs. Greenwood and the surrounding communities are better places due to Edith's efforts.

Teresa Griffin

To be able to share my thoughts of such a wonderful

person as Edith Childs, is again, most delightful. It has been many years of our acquaintance, and I must say that as the years have increased, so has our loyalty to our friendship.

Edith is the same. I have found that position has not affected the sincerity of the woman. There have been many opportunities whereas we have worked jointly. During these joint missions, I have learned a great deal under her guidance. Opportunities such as church functions, community efforts and political events as well, all have been both beneficial to me as well as the purposed events.

Mrs. Edith Childs has proven to be a true community leader. She is one that displays a total dedication to the job at hand, and has a refusal to the word quit. If there is a battle to be won, it should be placed in her hands to gain victory. I share these thoughts with so many other people that have had the privilege of spending time with Mrs. Childs or have shared in any type of event.

Kindness, dedication, and loyalty all describe Mrs. Edith Childs. I am truly grateful to know her and more than anything anxiously await the great outcome that awaits her. My prayers for Mrs. Edith Childs, is the great blessing that only God can bestow upon her. Her recompense could never come from man. The hands of man are not large enough.

Reverend Darlene Saxon

This is to let you know why we love you so much! We love Mrs. Edith Childs because she gives of herself unselfishly to her family, friends and community. We have known her only a little while. We have known her to be a person who has never met a stranger. She will share her wisdom with all she comes in contact with- Mrs. Childs is a fun-loving person, who knows what to say at the right time to help someone along the way.

Councilman and Mrs. Frank Daniel
and Michelle

Commitment is a word that describes Edith Childs. Whatever task she undertakes, she commits herself totally to seeing it through and to achieving maximum success. She's genuine when it comes to public service and love for community. We are extremely grateful that the Lord placed Edith Childs in Greenwood, South Carolina. Our community is so much better because of her. Our hats are off to you Edith.

South Carolina Senator
Floyd and Mamie Nicholson

I am thrilled to make sure you are the first to hear some very exciting news. Charlotte, North Carolina, will host the 46th Democratic National Convention in 2012.

Charlotte is a city marked by its southern charm, warm hospitality, and an up by the bootstraps mentality that has propelled the city forward as one of the fastest-growing in the south. Vibrant, diverse, and full of opportunity, the Queen City is home to innovative, hardworking folks with big heats and open minds. And of course, great barbecue.

Barack and I spent a lot of time in North Carolina during the campaign from the Atlantic Coast to the Research triangle to the Smoky Mountains and everywhere in between. Barrack enjoyed Asheville so must when he spent several days preparing for the second Presidential debate that our family vacationed there in 2009.

And my very first trip outside of Washington as First Lady was to Fort Bragg, where I started my effort to do all we can to help our heroic military families. all we can to help our heroic military families.

All the contending cities were places that Barack and I have grown to know and love, so it was a hard choice. But we are thrilled to be bringing the convention to Charlotte.

We hope many of you can join us in Charlotte the week of September 3rd 2012. But if you can't, we intend to bring the spirit of the convention-as well as actual, related events to your community and even your own backyard.

More than anything else, we want this to be a grassroots convention for the people. We will finance this convention differently than it's been done in the past, and we will make sure everyone feels closely tied in to what is happening in Charlotte. This will be a different convention, for a different time.

To help us make sure this is a grassroots convention-The People's Convention-we need hear from you. We want to know what you'd like to see at next year's convention, how and where you plan on watching it-and the very best way we can engage your friends and your neighbors.

Edith, please share your input with us right now-how can we make The People's Convention belong to you and your community?

I can't believe it has been more than two years since my brother Craig introduced me at the 2008 Convention in Denver. It truly feels like it was yesterday.

As I looked out at a sea of thousands of supporters that night, I spoke about my husband-the man whom this country would go on to elect as the 44th President of the United States. I spoke about his fundamental belief-a conviction at the very core of his life's work-that each of us has something to contribute to the spirit of our nation.

That's also the belief at the core of The People's Convention. That the table we sit at together-ought to be big enough for everyone. That the thread that binds us-a belief in the promise of this country-is strong enough to sustain us through good times and bad.

Barack talked at the State of the Union of his vision for how America can win the future. That must be the focus now, and I know so many of you will help talk about our plans with your neighbors-that through innovation, education, reform and responsibility we can make sure America realizes this vision.

Michelle Obama
First Lady

Mrs. Edith Childs is a very special lady. We have had many interactions over the past decade in regard to helping people in crisis. She is a lady who demonstrates compassion and care for the poor and needy. She is a person who manifests character, integrity and a courage that drives her life's purpose of helping people with a sense of confidence and humility. She values family and faith. I have witnessed her involvement and personal walk at work, through her church and the community she lives in. She has been deeply involved in planning, organizing and following through in supporting various charities in her community.

Edith is a special friend. She maintains a respectful reputation and a very significant presence in the area of helping people. She endeavors to communicate to people that there is honor and dignity in labor as she tries to move the people she helps to do the best they can to help themselves.

Edith is not a timid lady. She will definitely speak the truth, with love, and with the intention of building people up with their walk in life. She will make it very clear where she stands on various issues. When Mrs. Childs says she will follow-up on a request, you may have, you can rest assuredly and with confidence that she will check on it and get back to you. I am honored to call her friend.

Dr. Dan Flint
Greater Greenwood United Ministry

I have known Edith more than thirty years, and she has been the same but now she is seasoned. She is a friend, truthful, knowledgeable and most of all, a woman of God. When she tells you something it's a done deal. She is well-respected, though she does not demand it, she carries herself in such way that it jubilates.

When there was a summer program in the community of Troy, Edith had the vision to know that youth need positive input and guidance to become strong productive adults. Rural areas are oftentimes left out, but not by Edith. The center is still going strong with each year, increasing in number of youth and adult guidance, because Edith did not give up once funds became short. Troy Community is supporting the future of tomorrow because of Edith's vision and determination. This God-fearing and praying woman is family, friend, sister, daughter and Councilwoman to the Perrin family.

Carolyn Perrin

When I think about Edith Childs, and the attributes that make her so special, I say with conviction that she has a compassionate heart as that of Mother Teresa and the tenacity of a pit-bull.

Over the years, we have worked together on numerous projects in and around the county and state. I have found that when she gets an idea in her head it's hard for her to shake it and impossible for anyone else to deter her. If it is laid upon her spirit, no matter how far out of the box it may seem, nobody need tell her that it cannot be done-surely that adds fuel to her fire to prove you wrong.

While she is often misunderstood, I have found that when people get to know her, and become acquainted with her loving heart, one cannot help but love and respect her. She will be the first to admit, she has not always been the easiest person to get to know, and many people have been *put off* by her tendency to speak her mind... anywhere and at anytime. However, Edith, due to her upbringing has never been one to be intimidated by people, places or things." In that regard, she reminds me of Peter, the Apostle of Jesus Christ.

Edith is just as at home in the White House or your/my house- and she will speak her mind if given the slightest opportunity. One of her favorite sayings is, "I'm gonna speak my mind. They cannot eat me. All they can do is disagree with me and work against me- but I am gonna get it done." She then gives you that smile and nod of the head to let you know- and that's that!

While Edith may not, readily admit it, she has mellowed somewhat in the recent years and learned to pick her battles carefully. Nevertheless, be not mistaken, the bear that lives in her personality is merely napping, it is not dead. Disrespect her or her family or the disenfranchised that live among us and there will be no question in your mind as to how she feels about it - and *Lord have Mercy on your soul* if you disrespect her beloved Charles.

Edith is one that has dedicated her entire adult life to serving others in one capacity or another (most of the time juggling-this and that) and for that I say, "Thank you, Edith."

Nobody I know has championed so many causes as well as she has done.

While many, in and around our community, may not admit it, they would rather have Edith Childs on their side-rather than working in opposition of her ideas, plans and community projects.

Finally, you can find people that work hard for the money that stand to be made, but not many people are willing to work as hard as Edith for little or any pay.

As I often tell her husband, Charles, he has the patience of Job and there is a special place in Heaven for him for his having lived with a strong-willed and outgoing woman... my friend Edith. May God continue to richly bless you Charles and Edith as you continue along life's journey.

Reverend Michael Butler

Edith was a good neighbor and friend. She has always been there for me regardless of the situation. Whether it was because of health, sickness or death, Edith has been there. Yes she has been there with a smile on her face that encourages me and others to look forward to another day. I give credit to Charles-he had been wonderful also. They are the love of my life.

Geraldine Smith

A statement of recognition, appreciation for an unforgettable person of great character and leadership... Mrs. Edith Childs:

I have known Mrs. Edith Childs for a great number of years. She is a greatly devoted and a wonderful personality of Greenwood County and beyond. She serves as one of the County Council members of Greenwood County.

I find Mrs. Childs to be unselfish when it come to service to the community and supporting those in need. She gives her time, resource and energies to support many annual events in the community. She is a Christian. Faithfully serve her community by the expression of her faith, as a member of Morris Chapel Baptist Church, Little River #2, and Little River Association and Auxiliary. She is also a member of the health ministries of the association.

Mrs. Childs is a friend to all she meets. She is has a loving spirit that is well known far and near for her support of family and friends. Her participation in local events and her showing up wearing her beautiful hats has given her the nick name, Hat Lady. In general, Councilwoman Edith Childs is known as a friendly servant of the community and a dear friend too many, may God bless her.

Reverend Ulysses Parks

The days of the party line telephone and the black rotary telephones are now history. They are merely a good conservational topic. The eight tract tapes and the thirty-three record albums are now on the endanger species list. The world with the onslaught of technology, the Internet, cellular telephone, texting and tweeting is now at our doorstep. With all of the advancements of a computerized technology at our finger tips, in this world it is still necessary to have persons of integrity, honor, a love for the Lord and a desire to see all people prosper that is founded in Edith Childs. You are a very humble servant, one whom possess a servant heart, and epitomizes what Christianity and community services represent. This community, the county of Greenwood, the state of South Carolina, and this country, the USA, is blessing because you make a different in the lives of so many. You have worked tireless for a number of years with the back to school project, feeding the hungry, as a councilperson for county government, and your work as a nurse and in the health care field. You are an advocate for those that have loss hope or feel as if there is no hope. You along with your husband, Charles are a ray of sunlight in this sometimes dark world. As you will, we say to you, continue to be a beacon of light, that brings a ray of sunshine and hope in times such as we live in.

The question is asked; Am I my brothers' keeper? Your work as a servant, your love for the Lord, yields a resounding "yes." You, through your tireless work, the service you render, say yes, you are your brother's keeper.

Thank you Edith for the work you do, thank you for the person you are and thank you for our lasting friendship. We love you, and thank God for you:

Attorney Tommy, Barbara
Brandon and Brencis Stanford

It gives me great pleasure to write a letter of what we think of our Councilwomen, Edith Childs whom we have know for many years. My mother first met Edith at a school function in Greenwood County in 1960 and I met her at a non-profit organization 1998 and have being acquaintances since that time. We have had the pleasure of watching her grow into a caring and warm-hearted individual. No job is ever too big or too small for her to handle. She is always willing to lend a hand to anyone in need.

Edith's many public service activities include volunteering for Greenwood County Food Drive, Back to School Bash and the Barack Obama Campaign for President in 2008 which she has been coordinator for years. Edith has also taken part in sponsoring activities for Habitat for Humanity.

Edith is a leader, planner and strategic thinker. We have seen her take projects that had very few funds little resources and cultivate success.

Another prime example of her talents is the Back to School Bash that she has coordinated for the past twenty-years for the county. She has been able to gamer sponsors, volunteers and support from not only around Greenwood County but from across the country. I have been a financial supporter since the first Back to School Bash because of Edith.

Edith is a very capable, friendly and respectable individual who never seem to mind doing any task given to her. Edith is an energetic and enthusiastic woman who gives unselfishly of her time by keeping her monthly commitment in helping us to help others.

Edith comes with helping hands and a kind word, preferably describing her as a "Hurricane". She come with a big smile as she help with family members who are sick, not only her family members but anyone she know will accept her helping hands.

These are just a few of the major accomplishments that Edith has had with my family and the Promised land Community. Truly, we would not have been able to accomplish our vision and mission to meet the needs of the Promise Land Community if it were not for people like the *Fired Up Ready to Go.*

Jan Owens and Family
James and Gracie W. Smith

When we think of Edith many things come to mind. She first of all is a Christian lady, who is very caring about all people. She is a born leader, organizer and a great communicator. She knows how to get the most out of individuals when it comes to working for the community. Edith is multi-talented able to wear many different hats; with none of the hats being too big. She is lovingly known to most people as the *Hat Lady*. Edith is a great unifier of people.

William Parks, Thomas Gaskin
John Thomas Lyons, James Martin
Leroy Crawford, Robert Holloway
Johnny Carter, Melvin Jenkins
Nate Wideman, Junior Marshall
James L. Wright and Donald Wright

Throughout the years, I have admired Edith Child's love for this community. Her dedication to the people of Greenwood manifest in her services of love. Edith's years of service as council woman have benefitted the community enormously.

In every endeavor, Edith always wants what is best for our community. She always offers a smile, a hug or encouraging words to everyone. I have known Edith Childs for more than forty-years. She has proven to be a dependable, reliable and trustworthy person. I can truly say the Greenwood community is fortunate to know and have Edith Childs: she is an outstanding leader and a friend.

James Workman

A remarkable Lady! A one-of-a kind individual. A rare find. This is Edith Childs, and it is a once in a lifetime happening when one meets a lady who is full of grace and possesses attributes of caring, doing, thinking, loving and giving generously such that she is almost indescribable. Edith is always busy doing and caring for others. She knows that life is more than meat and the body and is always willing to share with those whose needs are greater than hers. As she knows the duties of the hour, she accepts the challenges of each and every situation no matter the difficulty. She is truly a leader and will always get things done.

My thoughts of Edith can best be summed by the following excerpts taken from a poem (Author Unknown) which comes to mind whenever I think of her. I'm glad I touched shoulders with her! Little did she know that I waited and listened and prayed and was cheered by her simplest word. Little does she know, I've grown stronger and better because I have merely touched shoulders with her. Little does she know, she has given me courage to work and live because I have simply rubbed shoulders with her. Edith, you're truly a remarkable lady!

Dr. Ann W. Morris

My wife and I have known Edith Childs her entire life. My grandmother, Ms. Maggie Gary delivered her in 1948. I was a few years older than Edith but we played together. Edith's grandmother use to bring Edith and her siblings to visit us. She has been a friend of our family. Our children are also friends now.

Edith has done so much for our community. We like to think of her as a God send because of her faithfulness. I have worked with Mrs. Childs on many Greenwood/Ninety Six NAACP projects and committees. Together we worked on programs, fund raisers, life and regular membership committees. She has gone on to win many awards on the state and national levels. Our prayer is that Edith continues to do what God has for her to do.

Joe and Dorothy Norman

Mrs. Edith Childs is a very special person and a very good friend. If there is anything she can do to help you she will. She has at heart the best for the people in the community and the world. If we need help with anything whether it is personal or business, she will do her best to help.

We are very proud of Edith because she is not only a County Councilwoman but she is also a strong, positive and honorable community activist and most important she is a woman of God. Thank you Edith for always putting people in need first and being the voice for the ones who have no voice and for giving less fortunate children much needed school supplies and safety information and a fun day.

Mrs. Edith Childs you are a phenomenal woman and a role model to many but most of all we are thankful to call you friend. We need more positive images like you in our community and the world.

Mr. & Mrs. James Moss

I have had the privilege of knowing Mrs. Edith Childs for many years. During this time, she has become a friend to my family and church family. She is a woman of good, strong, moral character and spirituality. Mrs. Childs is always willing to lend a helping hand to those in the community regardless of circumstances. She is like the merchants' ships; she bringeth her food from *afar. She riseth also while it is yet night, and giveth meat to her household, and a portion to her maidens* (Proverbs 31:14:15(KJV).

Raymond Adams, Pastor
Mt. Moriah Baptist Church
Greenwood, South Carolina

I have come to the conclusion that my cousin is truly an angel from above. She and her husband, Charles allowed me to stay with them until I got on my feet. I am very grateful to them and for them. I wonder how my cousin can manages the many tasks that she performs daily. At the end of the day, there are so many things done, and she still has time and energy to share a good laugh. She is one of a kind.

Stan Smith

Edith Childs and I became friends. Charles, and I were classmates during school. She was energized then and she remains that way today. I compare her to Esther in the Bible. Edith takes on a project and she remains with it until its completion. Edith neither wavers nor falters. It is a good thing that Edith is one of our own.

Lucy Smith Tolbert

Dedication

I dedicate this book to my wonderful husband, Charles, whom I love dearly. Also, this book is dedicated to our precious children, Linda & Lorenzo Brown, Jerome & Sabrina Childs, and Larmont Childs, my mother, Ida Edwards. To my special grandchildren: Lindaya, Lakeyia & Lorenzo (Zobe) Brown II, Jordan, Kequan & Cameron Childs, Deitra & Gregory Higgins, Tora, Tiara & Greg Higgins Jr.

This book is additionally devoted to a host of relatives and friends: Uncle Tommie "Jack" & Thelma Boozer, James & Phyllis Sanders, Nathaniel, David Sanders, Thelma Carter, Stan & JoAnn Smith, Jesse Pinson, Marie Jefferson, Tommy Childs, Miranda & Tommy Boozer, Diane Drennon.

I have taken time to thank those that are living and will have an opportunity to read and review this book. It is only befitting to thank those whose prayers have been an encouragement to which has also paved the way a long time ago for this day to come. In memory of my Grandmother, Mary Scurry, uncles & aunts, Odell & Dorothy Sanders, Joe, and Joyce Boozer, Willie and Grace Sanders, Marion Sanders, Lessie Childs my (mother-in-law), James & Clara Cooley, John, Nathaniel and Annie B. Childs.

To all my family and friends, who took time out of their busy schedules to be a part of the celebration, this is a momentous occasion. Thank you and may God bless you always.